OUTSIDERS

A BOOK OF GARDEN FRIENDS

RONALD BLYTHE

BLACK DOG BOOKS

For

Beth Chatto

ACKNOWLEDGEMENTS

The author and publisher most gratefully acknowledge permission to use copyright material from the following sources:

Ashmolean Museum (Robin Tanner), Christopher Barker, Cork Bricks, *Country Life*, *The Countryman*, Alan Cudmore, Caroline Davison, Simon Dorrell, David Gentleman, Charles Hall, Ursula Hamilton-Paterson, Clifford Harper, Helen Harrison, *Hortus*, Hunterian Museum & Art Gallery (CR Mackintosh), the Kurt Hutton Estate, Clarissa Lewis (John Piper), Glyn Morgan, John Morley, the Cedric Morris Estate, Stephen Morris, Peter Moyse, the John Nash Estate, New York Times, Norfolk Library Service (PH Emerson), RHS Lindley Library (William Hooker), RIBA Photographic Library (Edwin Smith), Yvonne Skargon, Humphrey Stone (Reynolds Stone), *The Tablet*, the Robin Tanner Estate, Tate Britain (John Nash), Richard Tilbrook, Anne Ullman (Eric Ravilious), Unicorn Press, Chris Wormell, Rachel Wren (Christopher Perkins).

*　*　*

First published in England 2008
Black Dog Books, 104 Trinity Street, Norwich, Norfolk, NR2 2BJ.
www.blackdogbooks.co.uk

A CIP record of this book is available from the British Library.

ISBN 978-0-9549286-5-0

Typeset in 12 point Times.

Printed by the MPG Books Group in the UK.

CONTENTS

FIRST GARDEN, FIRST TREES

My first garden was a plot backing onto some stables which now housed our goats. My brother and I milked them early in the morning before setting off to school. After the milking we staked them out on rough meadow land which had belonged to a Victorian brickyard. This was covered with toppling pug-sheds, ekes for drying the bricks, and furnaces for baking them. The ekes were hung with rich hanks of wild sweetpea. In February the claypits were starred with leafless coltsfoot and pink butterbur. Above our rambling clapboarded house were acres of cornfields gone to waste which we called The Tops. These were a forest of agricultural weeds where we made dens or lay low to read.

My garden was riven with greengage and walnut-tree roots which got in the way of my planting, and quite why I made it there is now a mystery, as there was endless land to choose from. It was liberally decorated with finds from the abandoned brickyard, beautiful red sunflower bricks, Suffolk whites and pretty bricks of all kinds. In summer they got buried in nasturtiums. For some reason I always planted penny packets of lobelia and clarkia. At this time botany was about pressing wild flowers in old wallpaper sample books and writing dates and locations in pencil. But any real garden cultivation at this period would have come from shuffling along the narrow paths of our relations and neighbours between beds in which rhubarb and runner beans, potatoes and cabbages had to knuckle down with roses and sweet williams. These gardens were drilled like a regiment and clean as a whistle. The paths themselves tended to be hairy with unmown grasses. The etiquette was to slowly wander along exclaiming with wonder, and then to be rewarded with a bit of this and a bit of that. It was thought desirable by country women that their menfolk should spend as much of their lives outside as was possible and a 'good garden', which was a family's most visible asset, indicated social virtue.

My garden would occasionally be adorned with a wild plant which I felt deserved to go up in the world. These rarely took. I did not much enjoy this child's gardening but, having started it, I felt compelled to go on with it, fixing seed packets on little sticks, arranging bricks and getting tired and unhappy. The only triumph were the sunflowers to go with sunflower

Out in the Garden,
wood engraving,
John Morley

bricks. How mighty they were! Although I had done no more than push half a dozen of their seeds into the ground, I knew real achievement. I can see them still, their plate-size seed heads and their bunting-like yellow petals, their sun-turning heliotropian faces and their sturdy grandeur! 'I grew them', I would tell everyone. What I also wanted to grow, although bits of them never came my way, were flowers from the walled gardens at the Hall, dahlias and especially glorious things like tall rudbeckia which I used to glimpse across the moat.

In retrospect I see that what I loved at this period was not my garden but 'my' trees. We start owning trees early on, no matter that they grow in the park or the churchyard, or near the station. They are ours. Ours for life. As with so much else, we remember best those trees which belong to us alone when we forget about rain forests or even Epping Forest. The statistics provided to arouse concern have a way of stunning it. We need to go back to simple numbers. Trees or people, even stars, enter our heads in manageable amounts during childhood. We are expected to be able to remember our first friends but what of our first trees? Town or country, it does not matter. For everyone there will have been a first tree. Once recalled, it will tower amid our early experiences. I think of the monkey puzzles (*Araucaria araucana*) which blocked out the morning sun for the two Miss Crossleys before they walked to their classrooms. And of the magnificent horsechestnut (*Aesculus hippocastanum*) which grew in the very centre of the market town and may well have been planted by Gainsborough's handsome nephew Dupont, and which was chopped down by Mr Chinery to make a bus park, both to which I made claim.

As for conservation, I was forced into this at a very early age when I was ordered to give five shillings towards saving a line of hedgerow oaks at Assington from being felled by a farmer. They grow still. I pass them regularly all these years on and feel virtuous and possessive. Halting woodland destruction was a parochial business in those days, but one which required nerve, for it was thought rather a disgrace to criticise a country neighbour. Petitions such as ours could be grounds for hate for years to come. Local papers are full of such battles. In the mid-nineteenth century the poet Edward FitzGerald railed against 'the race of petty squires' which cut down lane-side trees and levelled banks.

In a partly mystic sense those who owned mighty trees and those who lived in their shade shared a feeling that, if they truly belonged to anyone it was to their forebears. Trees have always been revered because they were seen by one's ancestors. They were planted thickly around hilltop churches to make wind breaks. The sound of them at service time, and the recognition that their roots held the dead, caused them to be worshipful.

'My' Suffolk pastures often grew isolated may trees (*Crataegus monogyna*), big hawthorns which became sumptuous and heady in late spring, and creaking and dark in mid-winter. The one in the meadow which led to grandmother's 'Vicarage Cottage' we called the Satan Tree. We would make a cautious little detour as we approached it. Better safe than sorry. I remember it because of its name. In retrospect it could not be less Satanic, indeed the reverse, for I see it as a white sexy mass which birds entered, and under which sheep sheltered, and which no one in their right mind would cut. Geoffrey Grigson used to say of the hawthorn that 'it helped and it hurt'. Its blossom, and that of the lilac, which Gran pronounced 'laloc', were never allowed in the house.

Another tree which stood all alone was the Big Tree on the bus-stop on the Sudbury-Lavenham road, a stagged oak on its last legs which stood on a humpy green. On Thursdays, market-day, we would wait beneath the Big Tree for mother, who was scarcely able to get off the bus for shopping. 'Big Tree, please', all the country ladies would say to Len the conductor. The bus would rattle beneath far greater oaks until it reached our hollow destination. It tumbled down one stormy night and a child-oak has shot up from its ruins. 'Where to?' 'The Big Tree', we say. Why has no one cleared the ancient trunk? Because it is a landmark tree. Landmark trees have a history of respect. Did the Earl of Oxford, en-route to his

Cottage gardens, Eriswell, Suffolk, Edwin Smith

woolweavers at Lavenham, say, 'Meet me at the Big Tree?' Politicians and hucksters nailed their posters to it. Bugg's Fair was advertised on it. If it rained, we stood inside it and let its brown dust trickle down on us.

Of course, being Suffolk, there were greengages (*Prunus domestica italica*), a small group of them, in everyone's garden. They were said to have been named after Sir Thomas Gage of Hengrave Hall. The trees were nothing much to look at, but their fruit – words fail me! You had to get to it before the wasps. I loved our greengage trees, adoring their skimpy branches and gorgeous plums, best eaten from the branch. A few would rot in the grass and would feed greedy insects whose hum became part of summer's music.

I 'owned' two woods, Arger Fen and High Wood, bike rides in more or less the same direction. Both were places of high romance. I felt hugely proud when Oliver Rackham included Arger Fen in England's wildwood. Bluebells and nightingales live there, as do boyhood friends and badgers. Trees felled in the 1987 gale feed its hills and valleys, and a cold brook waters it. It is a Shakespearian wood for lovers and loners. Scouts and Girl Guides camp in it, botanists hunt in it, and ghosts of brick-makers and warreners haunt it. As well as children, any naturalist can lay claim to it. It was there before the Romans and will never not be there. Or so I believe. And High Wood? When my Australian brother registered his company he called it High Wood, being homesick for Suffolk. But then, like me, he 'owned it'. To be factual, I never did know who had the deeds to it. I *do* remember that he and I were chased out of it by a gamekeeper, which we thought was the limit.

The mighty oak on Maypole Hill, Charsfield, visible from the author's house at Debach, Ursula Hamilton-Paterson

First trees included avenues. My parents spun along two avenues in the vicarage carriage to their wedding, each long and straight as a die. Now and then I walk them in an ownership-ish manner. Of course, like everyone else, I lost my elms. Bereaved elm-owners continue to walk the land in tears. Re-reading Keith Thomas's *Man and the Natural World* forces me to put my current understanding of trees in some kind of perspective. I grew up filled with respect for those first East Anglians who slaughtered forests in order to make cornfields. I am still amazed by the slave labour which cleared away the woods so that the crops could grow. And I never forget those early farmers who had to do the same thing all over again when they emigrated to New England. Keith Thomas offers me a philosophy for tree deaths and tree lives, for tree destruction and tree worship, and for my tree connection. Reading his book I find my first sight of trees – the possessive one – and a world view of them. Who shall I leave my trees to?

ON THE ALLOTMENT

I first met Roger Deakin when he came to interview me for a film he was making about allotments. It was the start of a long friendship. He sat me on an old wooden chair by the tumbledown granary and I began to rake my brain for an allotment experience, knowing that it would be remote and arcane. The camera whirled. Roger waited but was not encouraging. I was about to apologise for agreeing to be in his film when I had no part to play, when a whole acre of allotments which lay just below our house was dragged into my consciousness. I had tipped my allotment memories into the lumber-room of my encounters such ages ago that they must surely have rotted down into some useless compost where he was concerned. But no, once found they came forth, if it is not tasteless to say so, as bright as Lazarus.

There was old Billy with his homemade barrow and horsemuck. There were the multiple strips of dug earth with their many degrees of cultivation. There were the beloved huts which made up Allotment City. There were the bottomless pails over the rhubarb, the fringed pathways, the rigid rows of vegetables, the steaming manure, the benches belonging to the allotment parliament, the patches of sweet williams and pinks for the missus, the sweetpeas for the Flower Show, the monster marrows, the twizzling bird-scarers, and there, wonderfully resurrected, was as good a picture of a pre-World War Two allotment civilization as one would be likely to get. Roger stopped filming. He would be dead when I saw his lovely Allotment picture in the Aldeburgh cinema.

About the same time he was making it David Crouch and Colin Ward were writing their noble *The Allotment: Its Landscape and Culture*, a book which pulled into sharp focus more of what I had been telling Roger. The boyhood scene was lent substance by their scholarship. My allotments no longer floated in a kind of snapshot nowhere but lay between the workplace of the brickyard men and the lime-kiln men, the farm labourers and the silk factory women. They could be crowded on a fine evening. I now saw densely-sown parallels of jealously worked and competitive earth, and heard forks and hoes clinking, 'hooks' swishing, and male voices carrying as they do across water.

Allotments were all things to all holders. They were dream gardens, treadmills, escape from the wife routes, but most of all they were a club. A club which allowed its members to be social or solitary, whichever they were feeling like as they pushed their bikes from the lane to the shed. The latter were often monkish cells made mildly lewd with bosomy filmstars.

Their common necessities were a nice lot of squared newspapers and a wildly out of date calendar hanging from nails, a bursting armchair with mice-nests, and the requirements for a brew-up. The allotment-holders smoked like chimneys, drank strong tea and nothing else. They called to each other over the runner bean sticks like homing birds. The sheds

Autumn, wood engraving for H.E.Bates' *Flowers and Faces*, 1935, John Nash

Top Left and Right,
Norwich Allotments 1986,
David Jones.

Bottom Left,
Norwich Allotments 1976,
Charles Hall

smelled of dog, string, pipe dottels and boots, and it was a great honour for a boy to be invited in. 'Sit you down there'.

The produce which an allotment provided was little short of amazing. Potatoes and greens took up most of the space. Brussels sprouts were always picked from the main stalk, leaving it in the ground, and the branch cut with a little cross. This would sprout again. The allotment-holders were divided between the horticultural show-stoppers and men who simply grew food for their usually big families, and to be given away. It was part of Suffolk good manners to press produce on the visitor. The allotment men picked the allotment flowers rather like children in a bluebell wood, bunching the heads together in fat cushions. Asters were a favourite. Their currants and gooseberries ripened under old Nottingham lace curtains, seedbeds flourished below terrifying tin cat-heads with bulging glass eyes. Discretely at dusk night-soil from neighbouring cottage lavatories would be poured into a trench and covered with a few spadefuls of earth. Many months later one might see flecks of the local paper fluttering amidst the carrots.

The allotment universe – I am now dependent upon David and Colin – is a sane and honourable one. Its roots lay in some abandoned place, some village waste, some tempting soil between the tracks or below the gasworks where a man could feed his family. When these furtive efforts were rationalised into the strip vegetable gardens we see today they were met with astonishing hostility. Both farmer and squire were dead against them. Allotments would sap the strength of the field labourers, or create an unwelcome independence in them. It would be the clergy as much as anyone which, after the enclosures, saw how important it was for the countryman to have a piece of ground he could call his own, even if it cost him five shillings a year. Many of the early allotments were dug on church glebes – the old farmland which went with the priest's living and which supplemented his stipend. The Georgian enclosures pauperised the countryside and the Industrial Revolution towns and cities blackened it.

Thus in 1845, it became mandatory for villagers still applying for enclosure to 'allot' what were called 'field gardens' to the labouring poor. Disraeli attended a dinner celebrating the creation of field gardens at Bingley, Yorkshire and, unlike his dreadful Lord Marney in *Sybil*, who loathed allotments almost as much as he loved workhouses, was eager to see them all in the parishes of England.

The great Joseph Ashby of Tysoe lead a successful campaign in his village for the poor to control land which had been left to them in various local charities. Gladstone pointed out that most of the men and women who toiled on the land were actually garden-less, so land-greedy had their 'betters' in the parishes been. Once legislation had been introduced, the value of allotments hardly needed to be preached. Their appeal to the British soul was urgent. In 1918 allotment holders formed a union with the motto 'The Right to Dig' and soon they would possess something similar

Village Allotment,
wood engraving,
Reynolds Stone

to the social clout of the Women's Institute.

When Roger Deakin came to talk about his allotment film there were about half a million allotments in Britain and in some districts queues for vacancies. David and Colin nominated Birmingham as the allotment capital of these islands. The allotment-holders now have to hold their ground, not against the farmers and squires, but the property developers and the government housing planners. There is a promise that the East End allotments which the Olympics have flattened will be replaced. They are increasingly necessary as the average modern house-plot rules out the garden proper. One of the reasons why so many men are fat is that they have nowhere to dig. The terrible neatness of the world keeps them motionless. They long to call across their allotted portion of the world from shack to shack, to bend and plant and water, and breath the allotment air, to brag, to meditate, to eat what they have sown. Roger's film revealed some deplorable old chaps untamed by lawnmowers and edging wives, men who were addicted to wire-netting, corrugated iron, hip-baths in the open, and tall stories. Men who had escaped the property ladder by sinking out of sight into a nice row of double digging.

BELOVED OUTSIDER
ROSEBAY WILLOWHERB (*EPILOBIUM ANGUSTIFOLIUM*)

My first memory of this stately plant was of it guarding the black hearths in the Gull where the tramps used to brew-up. Taller than I, it somehow forbade gathering. 'I am not really wild', it seemed to say, 'just a wandering species like those travelling folk whose burnt patches I soon

Rosebay Willowherb,
Edwin Smith

hide'. It has willow-like leaves, hence its name. Its fresh purple-pink
flowers lean away from the main stem in a simple showy manner.
Eventually, for it too is a compulsive traveller, it will graduate from lane

to wood. Should humanity set fire to a city it will draw its bright veil over the horror in next to no time. Rosebay Willowherb is now as much a legend of the Blitz as the barrage balloons and Henry Moore's somnolent human flocks in the Underground.

I cherish it in the big bed under the ash tree, let it lie, let it gad a bit. For old time's sake. For it was not always a weed. Prolixity causes us to demote species. If pigeons were as rare as nightingales we would adore them. However Rosebay Willowherb has never lost its earlier status where I am concerned and I am glad that it followed the gypsies, and got about the world, and hid our barbarities, and never coarsened but stayed delicate, and remained prolific and lovely where we were mean and ugly. Indeed, I am all gratitude for the way in which it has conducted itself since it flew in silken strands from the herbaceous border to mask the cinders we leave in our wake.

Gerard found it 'very goodly to behold, for the decking up of houses and gardens'. He went on, 'The branches come out of the ground in great numbers, growing, to the height of sixe foote, garnished with brave flowers of great beautie, consisting of foower leaves a piece, of an orient purple colour. The cod is long . . . and full of downie matter, which flieth away with the winds . . . .' The French call it *herbe de Saint-Antoine* – St Anthony's Fire. The Seattle-ese turn it into Fireweed Honey, and Linnaeus recommends that its shoots should be eaten like asparagus. But every land to its greed. But let it travel, say I. Let it cover the wounds we make in the landscape. Let it hitch-hike along the railway and glorify old sites. Let it keep a pace ahead of us or bloom in our wake. And here and there, allow it garden room. Mine is on waving terms with the whitest of white Sweet Cicely (*Myrrhis odorata*) which grows towards the front door, and I am devoted to it. The Victorians tried to confine it to shrubberies but it always got out, went on its way, travelled the man-scarred world, seeing the sights. We deserve to find it accusative, but it says no more than, 'I am wholly beautiful'.

THE EPHEMERAL AND THE PERENNIAL

There must be still, even at this late twentieth century hour, many a small or great garden which continues to breathe the principles and passions of the kind of managed profusion which became the hallmark of enlightened English gardening from William Robinson onwards. My garden certainly declares these free notions – shouts them, some might say. Its antecedents crop up everywhere, on the bookshelves, in the outhouses and, most of all, at the back of my mind. I have become much attached to this litter and find it highly eloquent. Of course, my garden and those like it can be provided with a fairly exact pedigree by tracing their roots to Robinson's masterpiece *The English Flower Garden* (1883) and then carrying their development along to the present via similar well-known influences, but this would be too easy. As with all familiar things, lesser known agencies have had a hand in these beautiful creations. So many notions, some of them in print, some let drop by word of mouth, some osmotic, have helped to make 'my garden', as I still guiltily describe it, for although I have seen it very nearly from the start, and now own it, it can only be John Nash's. It was this old artist friend who planted it just after the last war and who, as well as its maturity, left to me the hundred and one pointers to its conception, everything from a Six Hills Nursery catalogue to a pile of Sankey's garden pots.

We came to our conclusion of what a garden should be in much the same way. As a boy in still rural Iver, Buckinghamshire, before the first World War, John had observed how a group of elderly unmarried sisters down the road virtually ignored the grounds surrounding their house and continued to garden what had been their childhood patches, cramming them with 'treasures' which in the best gardening tradition had been begged, stolen or borrowed from wherever they happened to have 'discovered' them. John Nash's eyes were opened and he saw that what his father called 'the garden' was in fact a croquet lawn and nothing more. My first true garden also belonged to aged women, a mother and daughter. It was dense with what they called 'their bits', a ravishing cushion of flowers and scents threaded through with winding dirt paths just wide enough for them to shuffle along and pat and fluff things into place. They pronounced flowers 'flors', which somebody said was Norfolk. The lesson which John Nash and I learned from these ladies was that a gardener accumulated delights.

Bottengoms, the author's farmhouse in the Stour valley

It was Clarence Elliott, the owner of the Six Hills Nursery at Stevenage, who took John Nash into the horticultural scene proper during the Twenties. 'I used to draw the plants he had collected on his expeditions to the Andes and the Falkland Islands and elsewhere, not excluding in English gardens, which he maintained were the best hunting ground.' And it was John Nash and my old friend Denis Garrett the Cambridge botanist who introduced me, respectively, to the world of the plant hunters. Not that I was ever able in either sphere to do much more than listen and look. All

John Nash, 1961, in his Bottengoms studio

the same, it was a green education which stretched back far before I was born and, as writers do, I have remained intrigued by having these direct links to the gardening past. Oddly central to such stay-at-home characters as John Nash was the Empire contribution to the shrubberies and flower-beds. Two of his close friends, and eventually mine, were Lord Cranbrook who, in 1932, had accompanied Frank Kingdun Ward on plant-hunting journeys in the Far East, and the painter Sir Cedric Morris who, every winter would desert Suffolk for the Mediterranean, returning home with precious shoots and seedlings concealed in his luggage.

But then the most untravelled gardener of their generation expected to have to keep some kind of pace with the plant-hunters. And in many respects garden imports were a two-way business, with works such as Mrs Earle's celebrated *Pot-Pourri from a Surrey Garden* (1897) inspiring the exiles of the Raj, and A.E.P. Grierson's *The Evolution of the Mogul Gardens of the Plains of India* affecting the Home Counties. It was

Grierson who had organised the floral background of the 1912 Durbar, just as it was Miss Jekyll who planned the gardens of Vice-Regal Lodge in New Delhi. It was much due to English gardeners born in India, like Eleanour Sinclair Rohde, for example, that a certain sensuousness invaded the gardening scene back home. Her *The Scented Garden*, *The Old World Pleasaunce* and *Gardens of Delight* introduced a languorous element disturbingly opposite to that created by carpet-bedding and ball-games. Nice, fat, battered old gardening books such as these lie around the house, every one a treat, and each a threat to that couple of hours' digging. Their inter-war equivalent were Marion Cran's *The Garden of Ignorance, The Garden of Experience* and *Garden of Good Hope*. I suspect that John Nash and equals like Vita Sackville-West and Margery Fish would have drawn the line at Marion Cran, although at this distance her work fascinates because it manages to convey the popular sentiment of her day. The popular exponent of horticulture whom nearly everybody read, the cognoscenti a little sniffily, was Dean Hole. S. Reynolds Hole looked like Gregory Peck and was Dean of Rochester. His *Book about Roses* became a bestseller and he used the influence it gave him to launch devastating attacks on the Victorian lawns-and-bedding-out gardeners who had levelled the exquisitely mysterious gardens of his youth. Quoting Pope –

Cactus and Succulents, John Nash drawing for *The Tranquil Gardener*, 1958 by Robert Gathorne-Hardy

He wins all points who pleasingly confounds,

Surprises, varies, and conceals the bounds.

– the Dean laid about him with a will. He wrote other testy volumes which I used to search for and give to John Nash. John's gardens, both this last one in the Stour Valley and the previous one in Meadle, were written about by friends like Robert Gathorne-Hardy, also discretely visited by plant-hunters and fellow artists.

Somebody arriving recently and seeing the tools, said, 'Do you collect old implements?' As these are in every-day use, I was momentarily puzzled. Then I realised how ancient many of them are, not least the roller, ladders and the right-angled fork for cleaning-out the ditches. The most evocative artefact was the little greenhouse which once belonged to Eric Ravilious and which came to John after his death in a flying accident during the last war. It appears in Ravilious's woodcuts and always looked to me like one of those splendid Duncan Tucker glasshouses which cost £14.10 in the Thirties. Alas, alas, it rotted, bowed, swayed and collapsed the minute I saved its last few panes from splintering. It was empty of all

Engraving 1935,
Eric Ravilious,
for London Transport,
with greenhouse and tea table

Ravilious's greenhouse,
Bottengoms, 1978,
Charles Hall

plants save convolvulus and mare's-tail but interestingly full of such archaeological items as a fragment of Rippingille heater, lumps of crazy paving – that nuisance – pesticide tins called Katakiller, Eureka and Corry's White Fly Death, and masses of pale seed-packets from long ago springtimes; Ryders (St Albans), Dobbie (Edinburgh), Allwood Bros (Haywards Heath) and Thompson and Morgan (Ipswich). John would toil in this beloved building for hours on end, smoking like a trooper.

But to discover just how astonishingly garden methods, philosophy and economics have altered during a comparatively short time, as well as this

THE GARDENERS' CHRONICLE

ESTABLISHED 1841   N⁰ 4768

litter and these gurus, I settle down to long, discursive hours with the journals of the time, the *Horticultural Advertiser*, Percy Cane's *Garden Design* and, best of all, *The Gardeners' Chronicle*, sixpence every Saturday during the Thirties and as revealing a picture of the nation at this moment as can be found anywhere. It is, of course, the final era of the fully-staffed garden and there can be no proper understanding of modern gardening if these (very poorly) paid gardeners are not taken into account. Whilst Ellen Willmott may have employed 85 of them and many a country-house a dozen or more, countless modest gardens up and down the land were cared for by a man and a boy, and the demanding nature of today's toil was, for the middle-classes, virtually unknown. In superior gardens young trainees were called journeymen and lived in a bothy. Their apprenticeship was long and severe but they could become highly influential authorities with a column in the magazines, such as Fred Street who worked at Petworth for Lord Leconfield and Mr Pateman, head gardener to Sir Charles Nall-Cain, who wrote regularly in *The Gardeners' Chronicle*. The Situations Vacant list made demands ranging from the tempting to the tyrannical and as the Situations Wanted list out-bid it by ten to one, even ads such as the following would bring an avalanche of replies: 'Wanted, Good Gardener, aged about 40, one under kept. Protestant, abstainer, no family. Understand bees if possible. By letter only. Upper Norwood.' The reverse of this was the swelling number of employers, hit by the depression, politely trying to pass good gardeners on to others 'due to reduction.'

A factor quite forgotten now is that one was seldom alone in any sizable garden; there were always men working – women too occasionally – 'Two Girl Gardeners wanted, age 18 to 25'. Both John Nash and Cedric Morris saw a good deal of 'girl gardeners' from the 1950s onwards. They included John's sister Barbara, who had a nursery near Princes Risborough, and Beth Chatto, who was Cedric's pupil and whose inspired garden at Elmstead Market contains some of his magic. Have feminists ever fully assessed the role of women in horticulture? It is a prodigious one. Lady Wolseley was aware of it half a century ago when she founded her college for women gardeners at Glynde, Sussex – just when Vita Sackville-West

A Garden End,
P.H. Emerson, *Pictures of East Anglian Life,* 1888

was planting Sissinghurst. And, proving that there is nothing new under the sun and *vide* Sir Roy Strong's recent recommendations, women with little gardens were, during these years, told to furnish as well as plant them so that they could be 'the Outdoor Living Room'.

An 'artist-plantsman', as John Nash liked to distinguish himself, tended to have nothing much to do with horticulture as public event although his middle-age coincided with the opening-up of private gardens by the hundreds to raise funds for hospitals and nurses, not to mention what sounds like the initiation of Interflora, when the Florists' Telegraph Delivery Service held a conference called 'Say it with Flowers'. He was far more likely to go to Stevenage or to the Physic Garden than to the Chelsea Flower Show. But he and Cedric, both possessing a wild sense of humour, might have enjoyed themselves at the 1932 *Daily Mail* Ideal Homes Exhibition at Olympia where there was a display entitled 'Gardens of the Novelists' in which garden scenes from Priestley's *The Good Companions* (*Erica carnea* planted in front of canvas moors), Galsworthy's *In Chancery* (flowering shrubs), Warwick Deeping's *Apples of Gold* (Mr John Klinkert's topiary) and Clemence Dane's *Author Unknown* (rocks and saxifrages) were on display. It was the golden age of the lending library. Carter's Tested Seeds contribution to this entertainment was a reproduction of that 'charming little square plot . . . surrounded by yew hedges and intersected with paths of crazy pavement' from E. F. Benson's *Mapp and Lucia*, this 'being fed by a gushing waterfall'.

Re-hearing, as it were, these intellectual old friends in their richly planted gardens, I note a lot of laughter.

Sempervivum, shells & flint, pen & ink, John Nash, *The Listener,* August 1933

THE SUNDAY KEY

Haphazardly in the conversation I heard somebody mention the Sunday key and I was back in Cambridge ages ago, letting myself into the Botanic Garden through the little gate in Station Road. The key belonged to Denis Garrett. Whether it was proper to allow Members of the Senate 'with their friends' into the garden on the Sabbath was a problem for Victorian Cambridge and there was a vote, 144 for, 129 against. The actual public would not be let in until 1950. Those who were able to convince the Sabbatarians that the plants would not corrupt their morals were given the Sunday key.

Denis Garrett, pencil, drawing Chris. Perkins, 1953

It was during my twenties that I met the Garretts and a family friendship immediately took place. They had returned broke from Jamaica, Denis, his wife Jane and their daughters Rachel, Lucy and Cathy, and on a bitter January day we all walked up Ballingdon Hill in Sudbury, somehow at ease with the future, mine as a writer, Denis's as a great plant pathologist. His and Jane's marriage had something of the Montagues and Capulets about it. He was from the celebrated agricultural machinery Garretts of Leiston, she from the equally famous Perkins diesel engines of Peterborough. They had met as very young travellers on a liner returning from New Zealand and Australia, fallen in love and briefly

25

Cambridge Botanic Garden,
modern glass houses

'joined the two houses'. Briefly because these mighty firms would collapse during the Depression. Although not all would be lost. Jane's father's paintings of early twentieth century New Zealand would hang in the National Gallery there, and Denis's 'Cousin Lizzie' and 'Cousin Milly' would leave their mark as Elizabeth Garrett Anderson and Millicent Fawcett, founder members of today's women's movement.

Trailing in the wake of Denis on the long walks which the Garretts took in all weathers, I gleaned a trifling understanding of botany. Nothing I hardly dared to mention in his company. He was marvellously gentle yet curiously formidable too. In some way august. He leaped up the botanical ladder like a kind of human Morning Glory. The young man who couldn't take the heat of the West Indian Banana Research Scheme and flourished in cold Cambridge and had his special chair as Professor of Mycology, his F.R.S. and much else. Best of all he had the quite extraordinary devotion of his world-wide students. Mine too. When in his failing old age I pushed his other chair round the boardwalk at Wicken Fen, I would feel myself bursting with love for him – for all the family.

The Garretts lived in one of those solid brick villas with long gardens in Hills Road. Most mornings Denis would pedal from it to the Botany School, or to Magdalen, his crumpled robes dangling from the basket, and usually dead centre of the streets. Time would come when the bike became a three-wheeler and Professor Garrett on his tricycle would confound the normal traffic. He came to no harm. Nor did he when he cut his hedge, a fifteen feet high privet barrier which lurched about under his ladder. His working method was of the simplest. His experiments were carried out in a back bedroom and his books were written on a card-table in the drawing-room as we all chattered away. A profound botanical scholarship enveloped him at all times yet mysteriously did not obscure him from either his family or his friends. When I first knew him I marvelled that Denis could bring me a cup of tea and draw the bedroom curtains. Or allow me to help with the washing-up after dinner in the rather dank kitchen, this being considered a mighty favour. When his wife installed one of the first washing-up machines he was nonplussed, and mourned the porcelain sink. I missed it too and the wary eye on where I was putting things. His colleague J. L. Harley F.R.S. described Denis's basic brilliance:

It was during his twelve years at Rothamsted Experimental Station from 1936-1948 that Garrett did much of his important work on root pathogens and soil ecology, which was characterised by great attention to detail. Each experiment was planned to a timetable which might straddle a month or two, with every important manipulation timed, even to the actual time of day. He made use of the simplest apparatus and glassware (jam jars). Indeed, later at Cambridge he was described as 'the last string and sealing-wax scientist'. In many experiments with cereal parasites he used lengths of straw, sterilized or unsterilized, soaked in water, or medium, or dry. These were immersed in soil or split to contain cereal grains. The replicates in such experiments often ran into hundreds, with the treatments replicated into factorial design.

Eventually he became the world authority on Take-all, the soil-borne fungus disease of wheat and barley and other field crops, travelling to India, Egypt, Australia – everywhere – to save their harvests. Nothing suited Jane Garrett more, who would pack a bag for anywhere at the drop of a hat. How she deplored my stay-at-home ways! My 'funny old house', my lack of adventure. Her artist father would cry, 'Time to move!' Once Jane said, 'The removal men arrived when they were having breakfast and put the furniture in a van as they ate, just leaving the table to the last.' Denis would smile tolerantly at this Perkins' restlessness and maintained within himself a kind of field stillness in which the only movement was that which caused the plants to grow.

The Suffolk coast was what Jane called his holy land. When I began writing at Aldeburgh the Garretts would arrive about twice a year and we would tramp the shingle shore for miles, Denis always looking down and the rest of us looking out to the immense wall of sea. The shingle plants were his native plants. It was usually wildly cold, even in summer, but people would swim and shriek. Winds tossed the flowers about. These were

Sea Campion, John Nash, 1956,
Aldeburgh Festival programme

Sea Holly, John Nash, 1956,
Aldeburgh Festival programme

enchanting, and John Nash would draw them and Denis would plunge around on the giving flints excitedly as old friend after old friend made itself known to him. This was the botany of his boyhood. His curious posture – he bent low without bending his knees, his legs wide, his face close to that of the growing flower – was one of loving recognition and of apology for not having been to Aldeburgh since last summer. His native coastal flora nodded chillily. Like him, it was intensely local, the Horned Poppy (*Glaucium flavum*), the Sea Pea (*Lathyrus maritimus*), the Sea Campion (*Silene uniflora*), the sturdy Sea Holly (*Eryngium maritimum*) and all the modest marsh plants which the poet George Crabbe honoured, Samphires (*Salicornia spp.*), Oraches (*Antriplex spp.*) and salt-lovers such as Sea Beet (*Beta maritima*), Blite and Aster. These too were the flora of childhood and youth. Crabbe only had to come within twenty miles of them and, in his day, that sullen shore, for him to drive down to it and drag the east wind into his lungs and cry, like Denis Garrett, 'I have come home!'

As a child of inland Suffolk rivers it took me some time to thrill to the shingle and its unique offering but I gradually came to see it as a distinctive part of my own natural experience, claiming a certain

Horned Poppy, John Nash, 1956,
Aldeburgh Festival programme

ownership, though never on the Garrett scale. He had actually known the people who had lived in the now drowned cottages which lined the road to Slaughden. Once we stood in the foundations of its inn and he said, 'I knew men who drank here'. I recall hoisting myself up into the Martello Tower. It was covered in graffiti, some French and tragic, for Napoleonic soldiers had been imprisoned in it, some the boastings of sexy lads. The nineteen-thirties penthouse on the roof still seemed to echo dance music, Harry Roy, crooners. But the all-over feeling was of squalor. Scurvy Grass (*Cochlearia officinalis*) grew patchily on its vast saucer-like wall.

Beyond or before Aldeburgh the three of us, Denis, Jane and myself, made for ancient churches or fenland ditches and sluices. Where churches were concerned, Jane and I were inside, Denis in those then not over-tidy churchyards where all kinds of wild flowers took cover from chemical agriculture. We would be standing on pews to search for signatures on Victorian glass, then being rightly re-valued, when he would burst in with a find. At Little Gidding he actually discovered a plant which was not on the Cambridge list. We would return to Hills Road like tired children. And then would come Sunday and its Key.

Denis-like botanists and historically-minded gardeners such as myself do much self-education in Cambridge University Botanic Garden, where there are no teachers except the beds themselves. Come rain or shine, we did the rounds, learning, learning. Its fascination depends on the pure observation of trees, shrubs, flowers and grasses – growing. No sooner was I inside the garden gate than plant-time took over, forty acres of it. The youthful First World War soldier, striding home from the trenches, with poppies stuck in his hat and bay leaves tied to his rifle, looks resolutely away from the garden glories which he might easily glimpse from his plinth. To the south stand the grand gates of the seventeenth century Botanic Garden laid out in Free School Lane on five acres of land which had belonged to the Austin Friars. And then came the twenty-nine year old John Henslow to occupy the Botanical Chair. He was modest and brilliant and consistently young for his age. Years later, when he had translated this mid-Cambridge garden to some farmland on the edge of the town, he admitted, 'When appointed, I knew very little indeed about

Sea Pea, John Nash, 1956,
Aldeburgh Festival programme

St. Andrew's,
South Lopham, Norfolk,
Edwin Smith

botany – but I probably knew as much of the subject as any other resident in Cambridge'. In 1828 a strange plant-struck boy named Charles Darwin came up to the University still wincing from the ghastly anatomy lectures he had been attending in Edinburgh and now vaguely considering the

Church. He began to join the unofficial 'at homes' which Professor Henslow held weekly, and more importantly for the world at large, Henslow on his long walks. The two of them became inseparable. Henslow set out his teaching as follows:

Whoever may be expecting to acquire a competent knowledge of this subject (botany) by merely listening to what shall be told him at lectures, will be disappointed. 'How to observe' is an art to be acquired by 'observing' and not by listening, or even by listening alone ... My advice to all who desire to master as much of Botany as may be required for a Pass-examination is to attend these lectures in their first year. In occasional visits to the Botanic Garden, during walks in the country, and especially in the long vacation, ample opportunities will be found for acquiring far more than will be necessary ...

Master and pupil, with so few years between them, were doing what the poet John Clare was doing not very far away, looking, looking. And seeing. Cambridge botany was at a low ebb, yet something unusual was happening outside in the water-meadows, in the college gardens, along the lanes, and it had something to do with 'the man who walks with Henslow'. In the late summer of 1831 the Professor received a letter from a Captain FitzRoy asking him to recommend a naturalist for a voyage of discovery he was soon going to make to South America. Henslow found Darwin and told him, 'I assure you I think you are the very man they are in search of!' Thus just after Christmas that year the momentous *Voyage of the Beagle* began to sail towards *The Origin of Species*, changing the sacred map.

I walked through the Botanic Garden during all seasons, and no sooner was inside the Sunday Key gate than plant-time took over. A water-course which had been channelled down from the Gogmagog Hills by Thomas Hobson when Shakespeare was alive lapped the far side of the Garden, as the Euphrates lapped the Garden of Eden. It also fed the lake. I would watch the lake from Henslow's walk. It is part of the original Garden plan and its surround of systematic beds, greenhouses and paths remains those which generations of Cambridge-trained plantsmen and women saw, memories of which they would have taken to Kew, to Pisa, to Padua, to Chelsea.

Having laid out his great garden, and having married, Henslow accepted the living of Hitcham, Suffolk. A thousand a year! And for a poor young parson-flower-man! His parish was grim. Fine trees but mean folk. Farm feuds, illiteracy, child labour, sickness. This would not do. He built a school, a sports field, and mended the slummy cottages. In no time, like Charles Darwin, his parishioners were 'walking with Henslow' and being taught botany. In July 1854 he packed them into an especially hired train and took them to see his Cambridge Garden, all 287 of them. They arrived at Cambridge Station at 9.20 a.m. walked the Garden and had dinner at 2

Victorian hot house, restored 2008, Cambridge Botanic Garden

p.m. at Downing College, then read the beautiful little book he had written and illustrated for them. He was a fine botanical artist.

Cambridge never quite got over Henslow's defection to Hitcham. Yet in a sense, because they had to tend the magnificent garden he had left them, they benefited from his absence. Some thirty gardeners now keep it in order, hoeing a skilful row between science and recreation. They say that the labelling is the best there is. I read it like a great book and am flattered when it adds a tiny chapter to what I know about some plant at home. Long ago, when the labels were made from strips of pine, they were stolen by Cambridge's notorious plague of jackdaws who carried them to college

Cambridge Botanic
Garden, main gates,
Trumpington Road

roofs and church towers. Blackbirds now take over from the jackdaws and
the garden is filled with their song and, sadly culled by tawny owls, made
limited. Metal labels stay firmly fixed these days. I try to master half a
dozen of them each visit, just as during my teens I would learn a few
verses of *The Rubáiyát of Omar Khayyám*, a poem drenched in roses.

Flowers and trees are powerful things and can challenge a strictly
botanical attitude to their existence. Linnaeus famously wept when, during
a visit to England, he first saw gorse in full bloom. A very unscientific
reaction. But I still find a visit to the Botanic Garden unsettling. It comes
from a confusion of responses to its loveliness, its rationality and its
democracy. It attacks both mind and heart, and all four senses. Buttercups
and orchids. And there is decorum. No bikes, no joggers, no transistors, no
unaccompanied children, no games, no fooling about. For this is where
humanity must measure itself against an immeasurable universe of plants.
Plant ethics, plant law, plant beauty.

One of my favourite beds is the Time Garden where plants grow in strict

The lake and arboretum from the limestone rock garden, Cambridge Botanic Garden

chronological order according to their introduction to these islands. They were carried here by birds, by princes, by empire men, by cooks, by accident, by law and by collectors. Shiploads arrived during the seventeenth century when the Suffolk gardener John Tradescant went to Virginia. Missionaries, merchants, artists, soldiers all came home with pockets full of seeds. But when I flew to Australia, it was, 'Turn out your pockets'. Once I sat next to a woman from Sydney who was licensed to bring in some wild flower seeds from Gloucestershire. Walking in the bush with my nephew Stuart I learned how many indigenous Australian plants went straight to Linnean names with no common name in between. And then came the wonder of the Sydney Botanic Garden which, what with the heat and what with the cockatoos, should have made me think of Cambridge less devotedly. But it did not. Instead I remembered the youthful Denis Garrett's first steps as a plant pathologist at the Waite Research Institute in South Australia in 1929. Did he hear the dull rise and fall of the North Sea on the Aldeburgh shingle, like those oceanic calls one hears in a shell? What was apparent even then was that his choice of soil-borne plant pathogens as a specialist subject to which he would devote his life possessed a richness and fascination for him which, when we met, was shaping his personality. This apart, he was in communion as it were with every flower that grew, keeping his own card index of them.

One day we went to John Henslow's church at Hitcham. On the memorial to him, instead of the usual praise we were asked to read Job 29. I found it in the lectern Bible and read aloud,

When the ear heard me, then it blessed me; and when the eye saw me, it gave witness to me, because I delivered the poor that cried, and the fatherless, and him that had none to help him . . . I was eyes to the blind, and feet I was to the lame. I was a father to the poor . . My root was spread out by the waters, and the dew lay all night upon my branch.

In Charles Darwin's *Autobiography* (1873) he wrote of his Cambridge friend, 'His judgment was excellent and his whole mind well-balanced, but I do not suppose that anyone would say that he possessed much original genius'. But as a recent Director of the Cambridge Botanic Garden said, 'Without Henslows there are no Darwins'. And without Denis Garretts the nations would starve.

JOHN CLARE AND FLOWERS

John Clare was no gardener but he was a mighty lover of flowers. He declared his gardening failings with an openness which some people today might envy, when keeping some little bed and lawn straight is evidence of one's character. When he was thirteen his father took him to Burghley House, a few miles from his home, for an interview.

We went to the Master of the Kitchen Garden as most suitable for my destination of working in future in the village, where flower gardens are but little store set bye, as the taste of Farmers turns entirely on profit. It may suffice to say that we succeeded in getting the wish'd-for situation. One circumstance in appearing before the Master of the garden will show the mistaken notions of grandeur and distinction in a clown that has not seen the world. My father as well as myself thought that as he appeared with white stockings and neckcloth, and as he was under such a great man as a Marquis, he must certainly be homaged as a gentleman of great consequence himself. So with all humiliation to his greatness, we met him with our hats in our hands and made a profound Bow even to our knees as we proceeded to the enquiry. I accordingly went the next week as a temporary apprentice for 3 years, for I was not bound. I did not like his looks from the first, and to my inconvenience proved a good physiognomist in the end. So after I had been here nearly a twelve month, I fled from him, I could stand him no longer.

John Clare in 1828, Behnes Bust, Northampton Central Library, Peter Moyse

Further garden jobs proved to be no better:

. . . for I liked to work in the fields best. The continued sameness of a garden

Wood Anemone,
Royce Wood, Helpston,
Peter Moyse

cloyed me, and I resumed my old employments with pleasure, where I could look on the wild heath, the wide spreading variety of cultured and fallow field, green meadows, and crooked brooks, and the dark woods wavering to the murmuring winds.

The flowers of Clare's village, cultivated and wild, spoke to him

Hedge Flowers,
Robin Tanner,
A Wiltshire Village, 1939

seasonally and eternally at the same time. He was the complete flower man. He was Clare the plantsman and Clare the botanist, Clare the sharer of their soil, Clare who saw women as flowers, and Clare the young man who recognised himself as someone who too had a growing need for a particular place in which to bloom. All his flower writing is now in print and we see how it dominates everything in his life. Few writers, even the best garden-writers, have dealt so obsessively with flowers, making them a science, a philosophy and a private imagery all at once. Plants were John Clare's actual faith. Only plants could save him is what he came to believe, and in a sense they did. That fenny land of Helpston, rich and poor by turn, with its brackish edge and its chilly spread towards cuts and dykes, bred particular folk and other creatures, all of whom caught his faithful eye, but it was its plants which actually bred him. As a subject for verse they were no more repetitious than any of the other stock themes in literature which are used over and over again without showing any great wear and tear when handled by a good writer. Thus where flowers were concerned, Clare unblushingly repeated himself. And yet not. Something new grew up amongst his flower-name plantings. Eventually they were to be seen as one of those species-rich meadows in which a variety of pre-hay harvest plants form a collective wonder. If Clare had a garden, it was this annual hayfield. Like a lover, he could lie full stretch in it, sensuously to read and write in his case. It was from such intimacy that he was taught his botany. When in a mistaken attempt to help him they re-planted him a few miles from Helpston, he would have collapsed there and then had he not taken its flower calendar with him. From then on, even in desperate situations among the insane, it never left him. His list. Although he would say like the Psalmist, 'I stick fast in the deep mire where no ground is', he could also say, in a vast series of flower poems, that he was one of the most deeply rooted men that ever lived.

One reads and re-reads Clare's flower writing. It is uneven, extensive, dazzling, dark and sunny by turn. In it one sees the poet more clearly than anywhere else. And by 'flower writing' one has to include the trees, the crops and every growing thing in his parish universe. It is here that we meet his intelligence, his art, his joy, his sexuality, his wit, his tragedy, but ultimately his triumph. The asylum years shock us partly by the comparatively brief references to his family, the lost neighbours and his fellow patients, the latter hardly existing in his huge output of words.

Corn Poppy, Helpston, Peter Moyse

What amazes the reader is the botanical profusion, all of it home-grown in distant Helpston but at the same time, all of it safe and accessible in his flower-list.

> My wild field catalogue of flowers
> Grows in my rhymes as thick as showers
> Tedious and long as they may be
> To some, they never weary mc.

'How do you get on with the flowers?' wrote Clare to his son. No answer. This boy would die when he was nineteen. When Clare was that age he watched a loner named Thomas Parker, who lived in Ashton Green just beyond Helpston, botanising in the wood. 'It was to him', wrote Clare, 'I showed the first specimen of my talent for poetry. He was my confidential friend'. Again writing to poor Charles, his short-lived son, Clare said, 'I very much want to get back and see after the garden and hunt the woods for yellow hyacinths, polyanthus and blue primroses as usual. . . . How is Robin Smith? We used to go and make ourselves welcome at the Bell . . .' And we glimpse the poet accompanied by another fellow plant-hunter, their pockets stuffed with finds and each of them elevated to the realm of flowers. Whether they were wild or not, he never drew a line between those that grew in a ditch or those that were lined-up in the Marquess of Exeter's parterre. We have him writing to his friend Mr Henderson, Lord Milton's gardener.

My dear Henderson, will you give me a few flowers. I have been very ill and and scarcely able to do anything . . . I have just got a proof of the new poems to correct but I can do nothing with it . . .

This was in November 1834. Whilst Henderson had taught Clare botany on their walks through the countryside, we are to imagine that the flowers

Marsh Mallow, John Nash, *The Native Garden*, 1961

Spear Thistle,
Peter Moyse

he brought his sick companion would have come from the warm glasshouse. Not much later, and now swiftly sliding into depression, Clare tried to garden at his unloved new house in Northborough, but it was no use. Mr Henderson brought him plants, talked botany, talked fruit and vegetables, and of aristocratic walled gardens where the poet would be welcomed, not as a gardener's boy but as a distinguished visitor. It was no use. The letter had gone on:

Will you have the kindness to give me a few shrubs and flowers, a few woodbines and something my wife calls everlasting. Have you got a drooping willow and a double blossomed furze? My wife also wants a red japonica. I am hardly able to say more. God bless you. Yours ever John Clare.

Some ten years earlier Clare's publisher had received a copy of Elizabeth Kent's *Flora Domestica, or the Portable Flower Garden* with a note saying, pass it on to Mr John Clare. He loved this book with, as he said, 'its variety of plant names, its sound gardening . . . its detailed descriptions which combine elegance with discursive treatment of matters of general interest.' Mrs Kent had read Clare's just published *Poems Descriptive of Rural Life and Scenery* (1820) and was captivated. Inside her book she had written: 'None have better understood the language of flowers than the simple-minded peasant-poet, Clare, whose volumes [he had by then published his second book *The Village Minstrel*] are like a beautiful country, diversified with woods, meadows, heaths and flower gardens . . . the sight of simple weeds to him a source of delight . . . he celebrates plants that seldom find a poet to sing them.'

Did John Clare allow garden flowers and 'weeds' to grow together at Northborough? Did Mr Henderson, the botanist-gardener to Lord Milton do the same? At Northampton Asylum Clare saw:

Common Spotted Orchid
Peter Moyse

> The Nettles by the garden walls
> Stand angrily and dull
> Summer on them like poison falls
> And all their blossoms shun.
> The Abbey's haunted heap of stone
> Is by their treachery overgrown

In summer it is weed-killing time though, given a chance, nettles can obliterate history. Weeds in Clare's day and long before our chemicalised

Cowslip, Castor Hanglands,
Helpston, Peter Moyse

countryside overwhelmed everything. Gilbert White would look out of his study window and praise God for 'my weeding women'. They straggled up to the rectory to pull and claw. A Methodist farmer, Mr Stoven, in the mid-nineteenth century almost wept as he pulled red-robin and poppies out of his turnips. 'There is not a weed now growing in my turnip field but will come to maturity and yield its thousand fold increase before the turnip itself.' It forms part of the curse still lingering in the ground. (God had once put a curse on the earth after the disobedience of Adam and of course Mr Stovon as a Methodist knew all about that). He went on, 'A skilful and persevering hand is required to maintain empire over this department of natural laws and forces . . . Even though torn up by the roots and cast out a thousand times over, phoenix-like the weed obtains a resurrection from its own ashes. What a tyranny has been exercised over man by the thistle as the representative of the weed world.' In summer in Clare's village the crops would have been equalled with what its inhabitants called 'the rubbish'. The beloved wild flower, gone beyond human control, became hateful.

In the summer chapters of Clare's *The Shepherd's Calendar* a marvellous book, he rises above complaint.

> Hawkweek and groundsel's fairy downs
> Unruffled keep their seeding crowns
> And in the over-heated air
> Not one light thing is floating there . . .

But it soon will. There is a haunting poem called 'An Angel in the Summer Hours' which is set in the hot riverside fields just before they become blackened and intolerable. Boy meets girl but not within the usual conventions of Clare's balladry. Something more profound is happening. A river is usually thought of as a divide. There is a poem by Charles Causley in which he stares across a Cornish brook at his parents, who are having a

Dog Rose, Helpston,
Peter Moyse

picnic when he was a child. They see him on the other bank. They have been dead for many years. Join us, they say. It is only a step. In Clare's 'Angel in the Summer Hours' it is far too wide for just a step. It is the symbol of what must always divide his existence. It begins with the poet doing what he has always done, lie on his back among flowers. It is the penultimate moment of the farming year before haymaking and the corn harvest, and the countryside is covered with plants which are not yet 'weeds'.

Clare's garden and wild flowers both challenge popular folklore. For him folklore flowers were a blinded understanding of their reality. He once chose the now cursed Ragwort – horse poison – as the subject of one of his finest tributes to a particular species. In the glory of its flowering horses graze around it, leaving it standing on the cropped pasture like some blazing remnant of all the gold which summer brings. He refers to it in his Byronic *Childe Harold*:

> And see the wild flowers gleaming up and down
> Like sun and light – the ragwort's golden crown
> Mirrors like sunshine when sunbeams retire . . .

In 1996 Richard Mabey created his *Flora Britannica*. If we want to see both wild and cultivated floral Britain as Clare saw it, it is in this great work. Here is Mabey's entry for Clare's pub.

The Botanical Society of the British Isles (whose symbol is the bluebell) has organised a survey of pubs called the Bluebell or the Blue Bell. There is a conspicuous concentration of these in the East Midlands, but most have blue bells, not blue flowers, painted on their signs. Some have both . . . The board outside the Blue Bell in Helpston has a church bell on one side and a bluebell on the other. Clare, who enjoyed bluebells, bells and beer equally, would, I think, have relished the confusion.

Clare was transfixed by the fugitive aspect of wild flowers, by their trespassing into gardens, by their lowliness in village eyes. They were so like him. We are now recreating his cottage garden at Helpston. The present inhabitants will scratch their heads. Will it be like Thomas Hardy's garden at Bockhampton and Shakespeare's garden at Stratford, a kind of flower field perhaps . . . would this be right? Would this describe it?

PAGES FROM A FARM DIARY 1989

Midsummer was a day which puzzled me mightily as a child because it arrived only a week or so after spring. It marked too the height of madness. I think not of heat or of seasonal lunacy, but of hay, and of how delectably it permeated midsummer – unless, of course, one was a victim of its pollens. This grass harvest used to be as gregarious as the corn harvest when there was a run of burning days, bringing everybody outside. The great thing was to get it all done before the weather turned, to mow, make, cart, stack and thatch.

I am reminded of this midsummer race against rain by the pasture just beyond the garden in which the huge may trees stand stock still, and where hay has not been made for years. It is a hilly meadow with a stream at its foot lived in by a dozen stupendously idle horses. They banquet endlessly on trefoil, clovers and mixed grasses, and on Saturday mornings are sweet-talked by pretty girls.

There used to be a moment just before the old hay harvest when it was a crime to walk in a meadow. 'You didn't come across the pasture, did you?' they would say anxiously. There was a week or two before the haymakers went in when the meadows reached a state of scented luxuriance almost impossible to describe. Their growth by the river was so tall that it closed over our heads.

I have had to make two brief visits to London, where I have never lived more than four consecutive days. The sun blazes and there are tar-bubbles on the road. Between research, I walk about staring at façades and faces.

Flowers of the
Hayfield,
Robin Tanner,
Wiltshire Village,
1939

The trees are often incredibly tall, like those in Gainsborough portraits. I look at paintings; it is a ritual.

I think of centuries of eyes levelling with those which glance from the frame, and of Francis Kilvert in Dulwich Gallery on Midsummer Day, 1876. He, naturally, stares at 'Rembrandt's immortal servant girl [who] still leaned on her round white arms a-smiling from the window and smiled for three hundred years since that summer's day when her master drew her portrait and made her immortal, imperishable and ever young [Kilvert was 36 and would be dead before he was 40]. The Oriental-looking Spanish flower girl still offered her flowers for sale. The Spanish boys still laughed audibly and went on with their game, and Aelbert Cuyp's cows grouped on a knoll at sunset stood or lay about in the evening glow chewing the cud and looking placidly over the wide level pastures of Holland.'

At home, best-kept-villaging goes on apace, and heaven help those who let the side down. A long time ago I had to help judge this wearing event, but as the car swept on through one familiar Suffolk parish to the next, and all of them absurdly tidied-up to the point of hardly daring to breathe, like a child for a special occasion, I found myself losing my critical bearings. It is the Feast of the Blessed Lawnmower.

Fêtes, too, abound. But I quite like these, and where ours is concerned would never have the letters 'E.F.' put after my name. I once read of a subscription list which contained 'Colonel Smith, £5 – E.F.' and 'Mrs MacDonald, £10 – E.F.' (Excused Fête). Tradition is the key to a successful village fête. Snapping canvas, excellent teas, stalls piled with bargains and a not too-bullying master of ceremonies.

I no longer visit the county shows, which I now find overwhelming with their permanent grounds, crashing bands and royalty dropping in by helicopter. One needs super-human energy to do the rural Season, as one glance at any June edition of a county newspaper would prove.

The gooseberry bushes are very old, never pruned and fruit profusely. They rise from impacted primroses, and have done ever since I can remember, and are so called because geese enjoyed them. The ancient jam on the larder shelf is labelled 'Goosegog'. Gooseberries are red, yellow, green and white, and have outrageous names such as Dan's Mistake, Miss Bold, High Sheriff, Rumbullion, Shiner and Adam's Snowball. I have never had either the skill or the temerity to discover what mine are. All four colours are locked together in a cruel thicket, and gathering them with minimal pain requires my reading spectacles and much care.

The fallen gale trees which have not been sawn-up thrive horizontally and are comfortable with roosting pheasants at dusk. Midsummer evenings, and indeed midnights, in the garden and by the field edge are an enchantment. One seems to be smelling the sun as well as feeling the warmth of its retained presence. There are lots of foxes and rabbits.

Old farms stay firmly isolated and islanded. My house listens impassively to distant amusements and crafts, cricket, remote dances, cries, none of them its business. It gapes wide to the landscape in hot late June, creaks with the heat and becomes a through-path for all kinds of creatures, not to mention a site for a particularly vigorous convolvulus which annually creeps through the brick floor of the kitchen and is not noticed until it begins to climb our corner cupboard.

Geoffrey Grigson said that bindweed has more blasphemy expended on it than all the other weeds of Britain. We called its flowers 'lamps' as children, and I have a tolerance of it springing from the days when I was innocent of its insidious ways.

The blissful thing about midsummer is that it is the start of summer, which is never a holiday for me but one of the best times for working. Its promotion of so much ease and indolence and sensuousness, creates a climate in which I get a lot done.

A month into autumn. Reading the October entries in diaries which go back for centuries, I find myself heartened by the sameness of the now and then. To listen to some of today's rural pundits one would think that these

September, John Nash, *Benham's Calendar*, 1958

51

Harvest Festival,
Sutterton, Lincolnshi
Edwin Smith, 1956

islands had lost their natural bearings. The diarists grow pleasurably sad at the prospect of dying leaves and light. I am struck by one aspect of this delight which is certainly unlike ours – the enjoyment of soft, grey days.

They don't mean Jane Austen's 'nice muggy weather', although I am very fond of this too, but that exhilaratingly fresh monochrome created by mild winds and dense scudding skies. The last foliage burns particularly bright against it. At night the bedroom windows are open upon a benevolent tempest which rocks the valley trees and trumpets down the chimneys. With a bit of luck it will wrench away the dead branches still dangling high up on the line of oaks mutilated by *the* gale. All summer they have swung and groaned. Summer indeed has masked the ruin.

The harvest has been what we call 'middling', although in much of the world it would have been seen as riches untold. The fields are ploughed and drilled, and already faintly verdant. The swiftness of this turn-around is almost too much for the gulls, fretful, ravenous, angelic creatures which feed in turmoil.

Our three villages form a united benefice, and so, of course, we have three harvest festivals – what incumbent ever believed that he would get away with a joint celebration? But I am all for such individualism. An English (Scottish and Welsh too) village is the nation's most distinctive entity, so for us one priest but otherwise three of everything. The vegetables, fruit and flowers are less exuberant, less naïve, than when I was a child, but the rich enclosed scent is just the same. What is different is that I can ask for – and get – cheques for the flooded villages of the East.

All three churches stand on heights above the Stour and the Colne and have classic pastoral views. Below them are the cornfields and water-meadows of John Constable and Thomas Gainsborough. October is for remembering one of my favourite sad sayings, the poet Jeremiah's: 'The harvest is passed, the summer is ended, and we are not saved.'

Farming is changing. First there was the reduction in dairying, now there is the movement to grow less corn and much talk of alternatives, some of them highly fanciful. The great dread is the housing developer. Returning from a visit to Australia, I contrast some of the new estates there with those beginning to fill-in some of the rural corners of East Anglia, and wonder at the sparsity of ornament, the mechanical proportions and the rotten little gardens. Do the buyers want such houses, or do they just have to have them?

Who built my house, during the Reformation maybe? I search its massive hodgepodge of plaster and wood for graffiti, the name of some old farmer or the scribbles of children. But all I find, tucked into a brick, is a 'Tenners' cigarette-box with the pencilled report, 'Feb. 19th 1937 painted outside of this House and Distempered inside. H. W. Spooner and B. Welford. Nayland and Boxted'.

I am invited to a birthday party. This farmer is 90, a Scot from Ayrshire, one of the many who made his way south before the First World War. He can remember the sound of the kicking of the plough-horses on the train, also the 'farmers' ordinary', that solid market-day luncheon taken in the best hotel in towns such as Bury St Edmunds and Sudbury when business was completed. His farmhouse is crammed with Anglian-Scottish relations. Early in the morning a commuting Scot had played the bagpipes under his window before catching the train. A few weeks earlier, this old farmer, who still drives, goes on long walks, and works, arrived with a Bronze Age axehead which his son had picked up in a field. It was in mint condition dating from about 700BC. A tremendous loss for the traveller on the high ground.

I also go to the wildflower nursery at Little Cornard. The best thing to do when plants become rare or near non-existent, or are threatened, is not to moon over the little secret patches of them which remain, but to collect their seed and multiply them. This is what happens at Sawyers. Since I last went, the nursery has grown by some acres, also by the taking-in of a Saxon lane. There are rows and rows of heartsease, scabious and pheasant's eye in full bloom. I have never seen pheasant's eye like this before. Botanists were always carrying it about England, and Gerard himself brought it from the West Country cornfields to those around London.

I, too, am carrying plants about, having come to a firm arrangement with the semi-cultivated intruders which have been turning my garden into a flowery jungle, things like cranesbill and myosotis, designated as 'thugs' by a much-tried gardening neighbour. My arrangement is that, if I give them the orchard, they can do what they like: sprawl, make mats – make carpets. My firmness has already paid off because all kinds of buried treasures are pushing through.

Late October is for walking. I climb out of the bosky dip in which the house hides and along the top field to have my breath taken away by a vast panorama which springs into view with all the ritual surprise of a jack-in-the-box. Saxon settlements, the BBC's television mast for East Anglia, and, glinting and disappearing, the river. Rivers keep you busy and on the go. The river-keepers dredge and fish and embank, cut sluices, mend mill races, grow crops of bat willow, and at the same time

Autumn,
wood engraving,
Country Life,
October 1988,
Chris Wormell

preserve some of the contentment they had as children getting soaked in the search for sticklebacks. I see an earlier self, too. The smell of decaying summer by the river, rank and memory-drenched, is a must for mid-autumn.

*   *   *

I rarely see in the New Year; it knows its way well enough. However cold or wild, or mild, New Year's Day itself has always appeared to belong more to spring than winter, so I go out. This is my celebration, to battle along in deceptive weather, not thinking of dates. What I am thinking this New Year

The Garden in Winter,
watercolour,
John Nash

is what landscape changes there have been since the Great Gale. The fall of wide clumps of willow has opened up fine vistas in all directions. Spires, towers and farms which hid themselves until one was almost upon them are spread out plain for miles and miles. The effect is surprisingly grand. But my line of oaks, with the leaves no longer concealing their wounds, has changed from splendour to pathos. Little girls ride beneath them, the feet of their ponies squelching in the deep mulch.

A barn owl has been sighted, though – perhaps mercifully – not heard. Barn or white owls shriek, hiss, snore and yap, as well as sail low over the night fields like Nemesis. Gilbert White says: 'I have known a whole village up in arms on such an occasion.' We are less excitable, and rejoice that this owl has found a newly thatched old barn to howl forth from. At Blickling Hall, Norfolk, the Hawk Trust opened an information centre to tell you how to welcome barn owls. I have glimpsed ours in a pollarded ash in a cart track and watched it crash away in a huff. There were nightingales here in my youth – another bird which likes a bit of human company, the evening lawnmower and radio programmes – but these seem to have gone for ever.

The agricultural press streams with herbicides for this, that and everything. They have war-like names. I always add suicide and homicide to herbicide to keep a perspective. New Year's Day is an important one for pesticide operators, for they must have obtained their certificates of competence by then, or stop spraying. This is the time, too, for farmers to buy a new tractor or plough, or a good reconditioned one. Their magazines are crowded with second-hand machinery. The farming mood is utterly changed. Even five years ago the present prospect was scarcely imaginable. It is not so much that the good times are over as that the old insecurity has been found never to have quite gone away. Incomes are down, and for some, set-aside – the policy of taking land out of corn production – is an uncomfortably novel notion.

A curious thing. Ever since childhood I have liked exploring bare fields, nose to the ground, filling my pockets with tin buttons, clay pipe-stems, fossils, and an astonishing amount, in certain fields, of fragments of china and pottery. I put this down to all that food being carried to farmworkers by their wives and children.

But, reading Rider Haggard's *A Farmer's Year*, written in Norfolk just a century ago, I see this: 'Today two carts are carrying refuse from the undrained town of Bungay to be scattered on that part of the nine acres of land which is coming for root . . . This compost, disagreeable as it is in many ways and mixed with troublesome stuff, such as old tins and broken glass, is the best manure which I have ever used.'

So these breakages which the plough turns up were made in the nearby towns. I knew that London burial grounds were sometimes cleared and the bones ground up and spread on fields in Essex and Hertfordshire, but I had not thought of the last resting place of cups and plates.

In the village church we prepare for the Epiphany, a feast of journeys and showings. This is strange when the countryside is so still and – despite being stripped and naked – so hidden. We shall sing of the 'gold of obedience' in John Monsell's beautiful, rather nervous hymn – poor Mr Monsell, who fell to his death from the roof of his church, St Nicholas's, Guildford, when they were restoring it in 1875.

The winter hymn without peer is Christina Rossetti's, with its iron earth, and water like a stone. This is what Suffolk was like in January when I was a child. Frozen milk being carried across from the farm by mittened hands with numb fingertips. And rooks soaring around. Now and then I get snowed-up in January and have to walk on the high ground to reach the road, but the cold never seems to reach Christina's iron dimension which was so common during my boyhood. Old farm diaries tell of frost destroying the wheat, but it doesn't now. Or rarely. They tell of 'smart' frosts.

The house is piled high with diaries, from Edward VI's to Evelyn Waugh's, as I have been writing a book about them. The first week in January is the testing time for diarists. Dare they – can they – write on for another twelve months? As my own diary never says more than 'Dinner with M' or 'N to stay', I remain untested. I shall write stories until June instead, and try not to forget what happened in between.

One thing is unforgettable: 1988-89 will be remembered as the time when thousands of farmers, most of them from East Anglia and the South-East, applied for set-aside, the Government's scheme for taking millions of acres out of arable production, and the beginning of the use of this land for something different. Only what? The scenery will soon show the answer.

*   *   *

Whether the season ends with a fall of snow or not, 1989 will be remembered as the year which skipped winter. Village friends have gloomed about it, but I have found it entrancing. There has not been a day since last summer when flowers for the house could not be picked from the garden and when the birds have not sung. The absence of rough weather has left the dead sticks and stems of last year's plants curiously intact, especially those of the nettle-beds, which have become a tall, gleaming, harmless forest in the willow plantations. The hedges too are a tangle of ancient purple blackberry leaves and precocious honeysuckle shoots, a determined mixture of what refuses to depart and what cannot wait to arrive.

It has been a busy home-and-away week involving plans for Mothering Sunday in the parish church, and for setting up a memorial to the poet John Clare in Westminster Abbey and, in between, long, quiet hours at my desk, plus bouts of digging. Clare is to have a beautiful engraved slate lozenge on the wall of Poets' Corner, next to the monuments to Michael Drayton and Matthew Arnold. He once visited the Abbey, during those brief years when he was fêted, a little, handsome, Scottish-looking farmworker from Northamptonshire who happened to be a writer of genius.

If England's fields could speak, it would be in his language. His is the purest English rural voice, and the fact that it reaches us via what he called the 'ship-wreck' of his later life adds to its authority. The memorial will be dedicated in June, and we sit in the Jerusalem Chamber thinking about who should come and what should be said. One of my favourite Clare locations is Barnack, in Cambridgeshire, where he wrote and botanised among the 'Hills and Holes', or in that wonderful open-cast medieval quarry from which they cut so many cathedrals, abbeys and fine houses. It is a wildflower sanctuary now and an experience not to be missed.

Riverside farm buildings are clamorous with starlings. Every now and then they take off in vast flocks which briefly darken the sky, making every possible sound from harsh cheering to spindly clicks. The pigs and cows, whose feed they have been stealing, and the horses standing gravely

Clare's memorial,
Poets' Corner, Westminster Abbey,
unveiled by Ted Hughes in 1989,
Peter Moyse

in the meadows, have given up trying to make their voices heard and ignore these bird armies.

Huge grain stores erected during the '60s, and now looking moss-stained and a little irrelevant, are sealed and invincible, and the starlings know it and steer clear of them. But they swirl around the weather vane on the cupola, an iron flag with the date 1722 cut into it, so wildly that it is a marvel that some of them are not spiked. They are garrulous Congregationalists, and already the scarers are automatically banging across the crops to dare them to land. I like their nerve. For them, to be alive in March is a kind of raging bliss.

There was for children a drama about abandoned cottages, with the garden flowers still blooming and nobody's apples and plums continuing to ripen, and with bedroom doors to open, wallpapers to be seen and decay to be smelled. I recalled this as I passed a small triangle of land by a brook with not so much as a brick left to show that this was where two families lived not so very long ago. On our long treks to see relations we were forbidden to go near such places, but they were irresistible and we would clamber up broken stairs, pick 'nobody's' flowers and fruit, and especially drop stones down wells. Between the wars vast numbers of fine old houses, uncared for and 'condemned', were torn down as part of slum clearance. Villages often reveal clues to where they stood.

Gravel pits were another magnet. They contained ponds with newts, and coltsfoot grew on their clay ledges. A persistent legend that a toad might be found inside a flint, and a jewel inside the toad, kept us chipping away. A neighbour put us on a more intellectual path, and we would come home weighed down with fossils. Suffolk is a flinty place, and one becomes devoted to this sharp, bright siliceous deposit which clinks against the harrows and shines from the church towers.

I raked the site of our Stone Age settlement with my eyes this week for the hope of an artefact and found a magnificent hammer-head. But it was not flint, it was granite. Exasperated corn makes its way through the flint litter covering the settlement, the neat rows having to break order now and again where the stones lie thickest.

I felt a different air in this once inhabited field by the Stour, something benign and less harsh than the surrounding climate. I make a point of allowing myself to be highly fanciful on a walk. March is a good clarifying month for wandering about in familiar territory. You can see where you have been and where you have to go. Thurber, describing his childhood, said that he had 'a trick of walking into himself'. I may do this deliberately when setting off on one of my day-long tramps across the home ground: I am not sure.

It never ceases to amaze me how it is assumed that one should share the general view of what should be allowed to live and what should be done away with. Over the past decade farmworkers, builders and visiting friends, thoughtful of my comfort, have all offered to rid me of my moorhens, my jays and my hornets. I am greatly attached to the hornets. They have lived here for ages in a brick recess high up the south wall. In

Abandoned cottage,
wood engraving,
Reynolds Stone

the summer they crash around in the grapevine or against the windows late at night.

I once saw the cat eating baby birds from a nest – as though it were a dish – lodged at the tip of the vine in a bouncing hail of hornets, but he was not stung. Neither have I been, and I have come to be rather proud of my huge wasps. 'Harnets' is what the old folk used to call them, and with hatred.

THE GIFT OF WATER

I suppose mine could be called a water-garden – except the water is never 'gardened'. It is part of the water-table of the River Stour which flows a couple of miles below the farmhouse. There are two horse ponds, a deep clear boundary ditch, bubbling springs and a series of tanks which lures some of it into the roof. This wild and domestic water never ceases, never dries up, never stops singing its watery song. It falls a few yards from my bedroom window with a silvery sound. Some of the outlying village houses still have rams and wells and like myself do not have to pay water rates. What we do have to pay is a strict hydraulic attention to our supply. My stream actually ran across the brick floor of the old kitchen in a kind of domestic channel. Very handy, they said. No having to go outside to fill the kettle. Or the copper. The vast stone sink into which it was ladled now stands on brick legs in a flower-bed and is grey with succulents. Generations of boys and girls would have stood in it on bath night, the towels warming on the fender. Now the cat uses it as a sunbed, squashing the plants.

There is a row of water-books in the library and all of them touch on water-sanctity. Although the Bottengoms water has never been known to run out we take modest baths for the pump's sake and frown on town guests who use a gallon to wash a cup. Now and then the Town Hall sends a tester to examine it. Once he said that other creatures, deer, foxes, badgers even, had drunk from the stream as it made its way to the roof. I approved of this but he did not. I sometimes watch the white cat lapping from it, a delicate business which always reminds me of D. H. Lawrence's snake. Taking water from a stream and not from the mains somehow retains its sanctity. Hydrolatory, water-worship, goes on. The early Christians saw fit to cleanse ancient supplies of their mineral realities by calling them miraculous. Not medicine but miracle. It is an old, old story, popularly muddled and in need of sorting out. My friends Rowland Parker and Charles Hall are exciting water-men who at different times have shown how facts are more thrilling than legend. But to comprehend the enduring mystery of water I read James Rattue's wonderful *The Living Stream: Holy Wells in Historical Context*, and so should anyone who goes to Lourdes or to the reservoir which supplies their taps. Did the farmers who lived in my house see my stream as a cure-all? Certainly it was why the house was built at the point where the stream ran into the horse-pond and the horse-pond flowed over to the river. A Saxon would have stuck his heel in and said, 'Build here'.

James Rattue, my water mentor, sees wells retaining their respect as much as their utility. 'In pools of water the human being first saw his own face, and could see the world mirrored around him; and this is perhaps the most surprising and extraordinary power of water.' Here is a gateway to 'another world'. James Rattue doesn't mention it, but no poem describes this more than the divine Thomas Traherne in his 'Shadows in the Water' in which a boy staring into a puddle 'chanc'd another World to meet'.

> . . . what can it mean?
> But that below the purling Stream

Some unknown Joys there be

Laid up in Store for me;

To which I shall, when that thin Skin

Is broken, be admitted in.

The three most important sites of Celtic hydrolatory in Britain are Anglesey, Wookey Hole – and Milton Keynes. When the medieval church measured sanctity it was all a matter of density. 'Thus the sanctity of the churchyard was denser than that of the area around it and that of the church itself denser still. Inside the church the density thickened until you reached the altar.' Similarly there was a 'Hierarchy of enclosures, reflecting the increasing density of holiness as found in churches, as one approached the water of a holy well'. Wells which contained mineral properties which soothed the eyes (sulphur) were known as sunrising-water. Water plays a great part in Christian ritual still. It is an essential element in it, from the going under of it in baptism to the adding of it to the Eucharistic wine, to the ablutions after Communion. And these days of

Stone sink from the kitchen at Bottengoms, now in the garden

Wood engraving,
John Nash,
Poems Newly Decorated,
September 1919

flower arrangement to it filling all the pots and vases. But every person, holy or unholy, needs must dwell near a water supply, as must a gardener. Often a saint's domestic or agricultural water would be become venerated. The path to it would become sacred – a pilgrimage route. This water taught its drinker deathlessness, or painlessness. It would be where, personally, the angel troubled the water for them. The Reformation and pre-Reformation attempts to close down the well-cults proved impossible in the long-flowing-run. The excellence of water one way or another over-ran them. God would for ever be reflected in it.

Once a year I wade along my ditch and rake it clean. I cut down the bankside growth and descend into a brick tank to my thighs to bale out the fine silt. It is a wet afternoon's job which brings a barely describable happiness and satisfaction. Should a friend arrive to witness this muddy man he will return home anxious. 'What do you think he was doing? Up to his neck in that old water business of his. He's like a child.'

WRITERS' GARDENS

So much of my favourite garden-writing has nothing to do with gardening-books that some assessment of its sources and pleasures seems due. But no sooner do I begin to list D. H. Lawrence's flowers, Cowper's greenhouse and the significance of the wych elm at 'Howard's End' etc. than the start of a vast literary-horticultural catalogue becomes apparent. This isn't the least surprising. For if the human action and contemplation which fills novels, poetry, travel and biography takes place for the most part within a cultural framework shared by the reader, some of the movement and quite a bit of the thinking is bound to go on in the garden. Gardens allow imaginative writers to philosophise, create social distinctions, be learned or/and lyrical, and occasionally amusing. On the whole, great care goes into describing them and often garden incidents in the stories of Saki, Henry James, P. G. Wodehouse – or in Patricia Highsmith – are more revealing of the manners and taste of a period than anything which happens in the house. As for the symbols and ideals provided by garden-makers, these are so ancient and so prolific, and so continuously evolving, that it is doubtful if any substantial poem or novel could be created without their creeping in.

Treating my bookshelves rather like beds, I have in what follows gone for perennial delights and influences, and, to avoid stringing along what appears to be the garden pages in every volume, been strict in my selection. Jane Austen's gardens must be among the happiest and best-known of all fiction. They are in effect all one single horticultural scene made up of the grandiloquent, the admirable and the homely. The reader is made to feel that he only has access to these linked plots and grounds as he wanders from Sir Walter's shrubberies to Mr Darcy's Pemberley, over to 'small, neat and pretty' Hartfield, up the drive to Rosings, across to the luxurious kitchen-garden of Northanger Abbey, pinery and all (described with real feeling by someone who must often have laid down her pen to tend the vegetable patch behind the Chawton cottage), and ends up at the poor Dashwoods' 'defective' home, honeysuckle-less and waiting for urgent garden attention. So essential to the dramatic and comic structure of Jane Austen's work is her inimitable graded garden scene that the novels would collapse without it.

My passion where non-garden-book garden writing is concerned is

Elizabeth Smart, author of *By Grand Central Station I Sat Down and Wept*, The Dell, Flixton, Suffolk, Christopher Barker, 1980

Colette's *Earthly Paradise*, the title given to a collection of her prose which contains a vivid, piecemeal autobiography, and thus a series of ravishing pictures of her girlhood in the Yonne, and of her mother's garden behind the tall iron gates. I re-read these Yonne pages frequently, wondering how they were created in order to be so beautiful, so everlastingly to carry the freshness of those 1880s Burgundian days, where Sido kneels on the grass, hat pushed back, lorgnette chain held between her teeth, and plants her cuttings, 'her hands tanned and wrinkled early by household tasks, gardening, cold water, and the sun, with their long, finely tapering figures . . .

'Don't touch'

'But nothing's coming up!'

'And what do you know about it? Is it for you to decide?'

In her garden-writing Colette achieves something which is far more difficult than it looks, which is to combine lyricism and hard, sensible information. Sido tells her daughter of the time it once snowed in July. 'It was a lovely day . . . lovely and warm. All of a sudden the wind changed, caught the tail-end of a storm, and piled it up, to the East, of course. Next came a spatter of very cold, very fine hail, and finally a heavy fall of big, thick snowflakes. Snow covered the roses and lay on the ripe cherries and the tomatoes. The red geraniums had had no time to cool down, and they melted the snow as fast as it covered them . . .' Ageing and famous when she set about it, Colette's garden writing is the literary equivalent of a Bonnard. Her mother's garden walls shelter 'a seagull, a stork with clipped wings, and a young cat . . . and some good friends . . .' Her gardens are liberties for plants and creatures alike, secluded in order to be goldenly open, like sunflowers.

My other literary garden is not so accessible. Not being able to take it in, at least not entirely, used to bother me, but its part-obscurity has become an added attraction. It is Andrew Marvell's garden. Not the familiar garden of

> The nectarine, and the curious peach,
> Into my hands themselves do reach;
> Stumbling on melons, as I pass,
> Ensnared with flowers, I fall on grass.

but the serious, lovely, now remote garden of his masterpiece, *Upon Appleton House*. It is an enormous poem, not so much in length as in what it touched upon. Marvell is employed at Nun Appleton House in Yorkshire as tutor to Lord Fairfax's daughter in what the poet calls the 'Nursery of all things green.' The Civil War is over but the wounds cover Britain. The girl has the horrors of life excluded by her father's stately garden. He is a retired general, she is growing up. The garden hints at past violence and dawning sexuality, and the poet's thoughts drift to flaming swords and 'luckless' apples, and he recalls Eden before the disaster where 'The gardener had the soldier's place', whose 'Winter quarters were the stoves/Where he the tender plants remove.' This hauntingly strange poem came back to me as I strolled through the graded hot houses of the Botanic Garden in Cambridge. There the confined and orderly, and brilliant, expanse of trees, flowers and grass, walks and water, is forced to accept an edge of roaring traffic, just as trim Nun Appleton cannot escape the fact that 'loose Nature' surrounds its floral precision. Beyond all cultivation spreads what

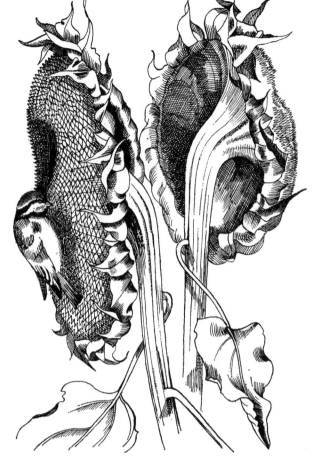

Well Entertained with a Sunflower, pen drawing, John Nash, for *The Natural History of Selborne*, 1972

has not been touched, or a motorway. Gardens, public gardens most of all, are necessary retreats, and we should boast, not apologise, if in a lifetime we have managed to add a little seclusion to existence.

The neglected garden, the going-to-seediness garden, offers much atmospheric scope to the writer and is a popular location for drama. Half-Anglicised Indian gardens are especially potent. There is an unforgettable one in Anita Desai's novel *Clear Light of Day*. It is neglected yet loved, needed but not worked. The Old Delhi climate all but slaughters it, but it hangs on, and the youthful remnants of the family compassionately observe its decline as they did that of an ancient aunt. 'As summer advanced, any pretence the garden made during milder seasons shrivelled up and disappeared. The stretches of arid yellow dust extended and the strips of

Angus Wilson in his wild garden at Felsham Woodside, Suffolk, Paul Joyce

green shrank. Now there was nothing left but those two long beds of roses, the grey-green domes of the mulberry and eucalyptus trees at the far end, and the water tap that trickled into a puddle of green mud. A party of parched mynahs stood around it, drinking and bathing.' Crimson roses are scorched black by the sun. Curiously, this messy, withering garden is not depressing. Had it been, the lives of the brothers and sisters who half-live in it would have been pointless. Penelope Mortimer also has a sharp eye for such decay, though this time in gardeners, in *Long Distance*, where a gross old

Ronald Blythe at Great Glemham, Suffolk, 1958, Kurt Hutton

man produces perfect crops of fruit and vegetables. And there are wild gardens galore in the tales of H. E. Bates, though blissful, voluptuous tangles where this writer is concerned. The novelist William Trevor lets the callow film-producer in *Other People's Worlds* say, shallowly, 'without being simplistic, there's a stench of lechery beneath the scent of lovely English roses' and that he would never allow the colour green to appear in his plays. This outburst is part of the foil against the garden-contained lives of Julia and her mother which are about to be shattered by that old serpent the pretty-faced young crook. Gardens as scenes of moral order and moral discovery are a feature of William Trevor's stories, and, of course, one doesn't have to look for the knowing why.

Post-paradise (Persian for a park) writing is massed with gardens. The world's sacred texts are full of blooms, pools, groves and orchards. Both Mary Magdalen and Julian of Norwich saw the risen Lord as a gardener, and 'gardens of love' have become a recurring theme for almost every major writer from the author of Genesis to Blake. The imagery of Eden, Babylon, Gethsemane, etc. – the lost garden, the fabulous garden and the garden of pain – continues to permeate literature, and the therapeutic benefits of gardening have an equally antique basis. Isaiah speaks of people purifying their lives in gardens and more than once describes them as a state of blessedness. These biblical gardens with their cucumbers, vines, roses, fountains and lovers were the sublime version of the colourful seed-packet illustration stimulus for me when I was a boy. I needed to plant my own and 'eat the fruit of it', as Jeremiah put it. And I am sure he would have included lotus-eating, had he known the expression. For this is amongst the chief pleasures to be had in literary gardens, the sensuous language, the drifting, the comedy, and the encounters with Yeats, the Ladies of Llangollen (a must), with Marcel Proust in Illiers or the Tivoli Gardens, D. H. Lawrence in any of the many gardens he wrote in briefly before moving on, or even in what a Wodehouse man calls 'these damp,

The author at Bottengoms, Richard Tilbrook, 2006

midgy, unhealthy, dangerous places outside very comfortable houses'.

Gardens have got into poetry and novels, and into literature generally for a great number of reasons, though chiefly, I have always thought, because so many writers, in order to find somewhere to work without interruption, have got into gardens. Angus Wilson liked to write outside, and so do I. And so did Shaw, Wordsworth, Clare and the young Thomas Hardy. Here is Mr Pooter working his way up from mustard and cress.

April 14. Spent the whole afternoon in the garden, having this morning picked up at a bookstall for five pence a capital little book, in good condition, on *Gardening*. I procured and sowed some half-hardy annuals in what I fancy will be a warm, sunny border. I thought of a joke, and called Carrie out. Carrie came out rather testy, I thought. I said: 'I have just discovered I have got a lodging-house.' She replied, 'How do you mean?' I said: '*Look at the boarders.*' Carrie said: 'Is that all you wanted me for?' I said: 'Any other time you would have laughed at my little pleasantry.' Carrie said: 'Certainly – *at any other time*, but not when I am busy in the house'.

THE GREAT GARDEN

The Great Garden fires us like touch paper. I give it caps because it contains everything which money can buy, taste devise, intelligence collect and skill can grow. Really wide herbaceous borders, soaring park trees, under-planted woodland, lawns which level-off into the distance, Henry James terraces, pretty gods and goddesses on plinths, flights of steps, orangeries, gazebos and, maybe, a view into the next parish or county even. And gates. And a crunchy carriage-sweep up to the portico. And water. And a summer-house and a winter-garden, and a tea-bell in a cage. And far cries and shouts. For the Great Garden is a protectorate and its spacious lawns will govern the visitor the moment he arrives. Each of these gardens possesses its own perfume and its special air. It causes one to walk in a stately fashion, look around in a rather religious manner and behave generally as though one has been allowed into paradise. Both physically and spiritually its sets the agenda for what must happen to you.

When as children we walked along the footpath which skirted Chilton Hall – there was an ancient right of way to the church – our voices grew quiet and we were on our best behaviour. Not because Sir Crisp English might descend on us from his battlements with furious cries but because his garden would be holding a green finger to its lovely lips. The other day

Hardwick House, Bury St. Edmunds, Suffolk, Edwin Smith

the life-peer who now lives in the Hall welcomed me in and for the first time I saw my first Great Garden in its entirety. Its buttressed Tudor walls, its glittering moat and bridges, its 'room' after 'room' of beds of flowers and fruit, its artfully enclosed sweetness, its girls on the lawns, its chasing dogs – and its solitary gardener, the slight young man who did it all, mowing, the digging, the upkeep, the everything. There he stands, Keeper of the Realm. When I explained to him and my host how we dropped our voices when we passed through their garden as children, overcome with awe, they smiled gently.

And so to Dartington once more, where the denizens of the literature festival, the poets and novelists, particularly those who, like myself, have been there more than once, are behaving as though they owned the place. Size counts. Dartington must be something in the region of forty acres. I begin by strolling towards Exmoor, nodding to the Henry Moore and to Mrs Elmhirst, turned to stone, and to viewing the Plantagenet

Walled Garden,
wood engraving,
John Morley

tiltyard turned to an outdoor theatre, en-route. After dinner I will walk it all again, sometimes with Jane Gardam who, like myself, is temporarily transposed into Great Garden ownership. Edward Hyams once wrote that the Elmhirsts, he Yorkshire, she American and enormously rich, thank goodness, created Dartington 'in the light of all the traditions, all the knowledge which had been accumulated during the long slow growth of the art of horticulture'. Two or three whole days of this! I tell myself, book talks interrupting, of course. And just before bedtime, with the lights appearing in authors' bedrooms, I head off once again towards the garden's far reaches, tactfully avoiding lovers and fellow guests needing a bit of company. Warm summer darkness in a Great Garden, with owls screeching and its scents intensifying, and its damps rising, and its order being challenged by its underlying wildness, but its 'privilege' staying intact, what a treat. In bed at midnight, I let all this blow through my open window. People pass by on the gravel below, talking not about gardens but Julian Barnes.

The great gardens of Britain are spellbinding achievements, as majestic in their way as any cathedral. Once through their gates, and their scale, colour, learning and harmony lay hold of you. You walk, look, think – and are changed. How was it done? I ask myself when I enter Bodnant or Stourhead, or Didcote Manor. How did this bringing together of grass and lakes, shrubberies, walks, species, views, architecture make so perfect a whole? And why should it prove to be so universally satisfying? For Monty Don finds every kind of contentment in every kind of Great Garden. They seemed to be more governed by confidence than rules. Each one is a truly heroic pursuit of pleasure and display of private tastes. And until the invention of the lawn-mower in particular, the hedge-cutter and stables full of brilliant machinery, they could only be created and maintained by an army of gardeners, thus they could not be as wonderfully private as they are today. Eyes were everywhere. One paid for their upkeep with far more than small wages, as one did with the great house.

Praise God for the gadgets which not only did away with hard labour, but observance. The bliss of having forty trim acres to oneself! Or more or less. Just the far howl of the chainsaw.

Undiluted pride is exhibited in a Great Garden. For centuries those who lived in fine houses woke up each morning to the delights of the world as they had contrived it. When Xenophon was shown the garden of King Cyrus he made a note of its Persian name – 'Paradise'. Britain's gardens, great and small, its window-ledges even, offer a pick of paradises. Each shows its owner's determination to lay out his notion of heaven in full view of his residence.

An exploration of Great Gardens might begin in London, where its glorious parks and other public grounds must be included. Thus Queen Mary's Rose Garden in Regent's Park and the forty acres of Buckingham Palace garden where the turf somehow stands up to the vast parties and an exclusivity just manages to reign, and band music does not quite deafen the birds. Toppered and tailed, I was able to slip away from the honoured multitude for half an hour to look at the royal mulch, the creepers on the walls and all the normally out of sight things. Nothing was trampled and this was the miracle. Compared with Versailles Buckingham Palace Garden is, well, homely. But to discover the epicentre of our gardens, both stately and domestic, one has to go to Kew. This is the heart of our horticultural statement. Once the Duke of Kent's home, it is a plant world beyond compare. Although it has a long history, Kew is always morning-new. In May Kew bluebells are so multitudinous, *so* blue, that they appear to stain the sky and land for miles around. Kew is Britain's collector and processor of all botanical intelligence. Species from every mile of the globe are brought here in order to be understood, protected and propagated. Kew is a plant library, a plant art gallery and the garden of gardens. Sir William Chambers' exotic pagoda watches over it and the mighty glasshouse is its temple. Crammed with foreign wonders though it is, Kew has remained resolutely English – and not even British.

Kew Gardens
Edwin Smith

Sissinghurst,
The cottage garden,
Edwin Smith

Hidcote,
Edwin Smith

Outside the capital one of my favourite gardens is the one which Sir Eric Savill made for King George VI in Windsor Great Park just after World War II. It is one of the last gardens to be designed in the grand manner. Many visitors to the Castle remain unaware of its existence because it is three miles distant and planted just off the Staines Road. It is an addition to a series of woodland gardens which over the years have been incorporated in Windsor Great Park. These gardens are so big and their trees – many of which would have witnessed Elizabeth I hunting beneath them – so superb that you felt you have discovered another country or kingdom. With their meandering mown walks and wildflower-packed verges, they are a triumph of informality. London's great gardens include Hampton Court with its green knots and twisting red brick, and Osterley with its vast greensward and Doric temple, its stretching cedars of Lebanon and its air of classical deliberation in all things. To understand what is happening in these gardens, for they never stand still, you need to stand on the front steps of the house. Trees do not just rustle here, they quote Virgil.

The Shell Grotto, Stowe, John Piper

The most popular gardener's garden in Britain is perhaps Sissinghurst. Its maker did all that she could to see that it would never qualify for the big league. 'Anyone can make a Sissinghurst', she is saying. And many try to, though fail in the attempt. A tall pinnacled gateway leads into it. It says, 'Go home and do thou likewise'. The tale of these ten acres of bliss is recent and very romantic. In 1930 the poet Vita Sackville-West, the hero and heroine both of her friend's novel *Orlando*, bought what was then little more than a clutter of semi-derelict old buildings and their stagnant grounds so that she could make a kind of garden statement on her own existence. This intention she confessed in book after book. But because of what she accomplished and described in some of the finest garden journalism ever written, she made it seem possible for anyone to do what she was doing. Thus her lasting influence. Vita Sackville-West has long joined the ranks of persuasive women gardeners. What would our gardens have looked like had not she, or Gertrude Jekyll, Theresa Earle, Margery Fish, Jane Loudon, Mirabel Osler, Ellen Willmott, Marion Cran, and a host of ladies not dug, planted and written! Rosemary Verey and Beth Chatto continue their mission. Vita Sackville-West died half a century ago. Here she is describing her famous White Garden.

The Palladian
Bridge, Stowe

It is amusing to make one-colour gardens . . . For my part I am trying to make a grey, green and white garden . . . I visualize the white trumpets of dozens of Regale lilies, grown three years ago from seed, coming up through the grey of southernwood and Artemisia and cotton-lavender, with grey and white edging plants such as *Dianthus* 'Mrs Sinkins' and the silvery mats of *Stachys lanata*, more familiar and so much nicer under its English names of Rabbits' Ears or Saviour's Flannel . . . There will be white pansies and white peonies, and white irises with grey leaves . . . I cannot help hoping that the great ghostly barn-owl will sweep silently across a pale garden, next summer, in the twilight – the pale garden that I am now planting, under the first flakes of snow.

Vita Sackville-West continues to haunt her comparatively small Great Garden, a lasting presence in her combination of twinset and pearls, and breeches and boots. 'Lady Chatterley above the waist, gamekeeper below it', said the wits. We see her earth-stained hands, the cigarette-holder, the long English face. 'Once of the noble land I dared to pull the organ stops' she confessed in a poem. Sissinghurst is the result.

In my own native East Anglia there is Oxburgh Hall in Norfolk, with its intricate parterres, through which paths run like embroidery, and Long Melford in Suffolk with its bowling-house – the one which Elizabeth I would have seen. Five hundred gentlemen dressed in velvet escorted her to this garden. And Blickling Hall, Norfolk again, is a rural palace with an orangery where the moat used to be. A rare rose named *Duchess of Portland,* the ancestor of our modern roses, still grows here. Blickling possesses a handsome remnant of the traditional English formal garden, of which that at Montacute House in Somerset may be said to be the peak. Its lawns, topiary, Spanish chestnuts and sequences of flowering rooms which open into each other have outwitted their Victorian remodelling. It is the enduring confidence of Montacute's first design – the triumphant union of architecture and growing things which makes this place so lovely.

Temple of Flora,
Stourhead,
Edwin Smith

Stourhead (Wiltshire) is to gardening what Mozart is to music. It was created by the banker Henry Hoare and his descendants. They had read the classical poets, seen Italy, known artists like Gainsborough and Richard Wilson. Their 'views' had to pass beyond the park into the surrounding landscape in order to show than no line should be drawn between an artistic cultivation and 'nature', or the countryside. Emparking, as it was called, had been a method of excluding the latter from the 'seat'. Oliver Goldsmith attacked it in his angry poem *The Deserted Village*. Stourhead is inclusive, taking in rivers, hills, native plants and exotic plants, rare birds and local creatures, and walks to suit every mood from morbidity to joy. It is proof of what a Chinese philosopher said, 'If you would be happy for a week, take a wife: if you would be happy for a month, kill a pig: if you would be happy for ever, plant a garden'.

The Great Garden instantly started garden tourism. It is made for visitation, though not for today's big business. And here is the chief difference between ourselves and our forebears. They showed-off, we pay. Though rarely more willingly for anything. Anglesey Abbey, Wakehurst Place, Petworth, Lanhyrock in Cornwall which Thomas Hardy usurped for his beautiful courtship novel *A Pair of Blue Eyes*, there they are, perfectly kept Edens with no flaming swords to keep us out. Wallington (Cumbria), Mount Steward (County Down), Tatton Park (Cheshire), Saltram (Devon), seemingly a Great Garden every few miles. Tea too. And each one an education and a rest.

THE ROSES AT BOTTENGOMS FARM

The rose has been all things to all men and to all ages. Naturally, it knows nothing of this. All that the rose knows is what any plant knows, that it has little to do with human love, divine symbols, art, science, poetry or emblems. Throughout history every practical, emotional, religious and imaginative faculty has been imposed on this flower. But with shape, hue and scent all combining to exact our adoration, it is no wonder that over the centuries we should in so many different ways have given it eminence above every other bloom. Thus providing it with a legend – countless legends to be exact – which allows it to take precedence in the garden. All this rose worship has made for endless rose tales, rose faith and rose truths. We can be passionate and mystical about roses, romantic, sexy, anything we fancy. The rose can take it. The rose historian Graham Rose says that its image is always one of excess. And of course roses aren't what they used to be. Many modern roses are 'harsh, scentless and garish' – Robin Lane Fox. Dean Hole of Rochester told the Edwardians that life wasn't worth living without roses. The Church called Mary the Rose of all Roses and its string of prayer-beads a Rosary. William Blake saw the corruption at its heart. Music and literature glorified it in Strauss's *Rosenkavalier*, Nijinsky's *Spectre de la Rose* and the poets of the Middle Ages's *Roman de la Rose*. And one could go on for volumes.

Plaque at Bottengoms with
Gloire de Dijon rose

The other day I visited my roses in turn and found *La Reine Victoria* by an oak, *Duke of Wellington* on a wall, *Leda* (marvellously white) near the seat, *Tuscany* on a pear-tree, *Charles de Mille* being strangled by *vinca*, *Zephrine Drouin* where Christine Nash used to doze, *Alba* near the holly hedge, *William Lobb* by the oil tank, pink *Celestine*, stripey *York and Lancaster* and dark *Nuit St George* all doing well, the *Five Brothers* rather ill, and John Nash's favourite *Gloire de Dijon* staring through the study window. Tony Venison, long the great garden editor of *Country Life* now and then brings me roses plus a note.

Rosa hemisphaelica from Persia, yellow flowers, hot and dry. Brown, very spiny stems.

Rosa foliosa from North Carolina. Good autumn colour. Green stems, very few thorns.

I am about to come in when *Maiden's Blush* and *Cardinal Richelieu*, dark as dark, and *Rosa Pimpinellifolia*, and the *Sweet Briar* in the orchard murmur, 'What about us?' And what about *Sir Cedric Morris* who touched the sky and scratched everyone for miles? And who suddenly died! Should he be replaced? If only for old time's sake? I used to see it in Cedric's garden, a rose as big as all the old sheds which it smothered, cruel and lovely, and greenish-white, a rose out to get you.

'There's one other flower in the garden that can move about like you' said the Rose . . . 'but she's more bushy than you are.'

'Is she like me?' Alice asked eagerly, for the thought crossed her mind: 'There's another little girl in the garden somewhere!'

'Well, she has the same awkward shape as you,' the Rose said, 'but she's redder – and her petals are shorter, I think.'

'They're done up close like a dahlia,' said the Tiger Lily; 'not tumbled about like yours.'

'But that's not *your* fault,' the Rose added kindly: you're beginning to fade, you know – and then one cannot help one's petals getting a little untidy.'

Alice didn't like this idea at all; so to change the subject, she asked, 'Does she ever come out here?'

'I dare say you'll see her soon,' said the Rose. 'She's one of the kind that has nine spikes, you know.'

'Where does she wear them?' Alice asked with some curiosity.

'Why, all round her head, of course,' the Rose replied. 'I was wondering why *you* hadn't got some too. I thought it was the regular rule.'

'She's coming!' cried the Larkspur. 'I hear her footstep, thump, thump along the gravel walk!'

Alice looked round eagerly, and found that it was the Red Queen.

(The Queen of Hearts' penalty for planting white roses instead of red was – death!)

Rosary. Originally this word denoted a rosarium, or rose garden . . . an abode of spiritual beauty and purity. A Latin verse attributed to St Bernard (1091-1153) suggests that the link between the rose and prayers to the Virgin Mary already existed in the 12th century:

Ave, salve, gaude, vale
A Maria, non vernale

Garden Flowers,
John Nash,
The Curious Gardener, 1932

Old Fashioned Roses,
John Nash,
The Tranquil Gardener, 1958

Sed de Rosis spiritale

Tibi plecto nunc crinale

De Rosarum flosculis

(Hail and flourish, rejoice and be strong,

O Mary, no springtime wreath of rosebuds do I entwine

but, for you, from the roses, a spiritual one.)

'The early rosaries were made up of rose petals, strung together and, later, rose-hips may have been used instead.'

John Fisher, *The Companion to Roses*, (1986)

Gloire de Dijon rose (above), Campanula and the Cabbage rose (below), Bottengoms

Bottengoms Roses
Top left - *John Clare* (Peter Moyse),
Top right - *Gloire de Dijon*
Bottom left - *Rosa Mundi* and Nepeta (Helen Harrison)

Bottengoms Garden
Top left - Rosa *William Lobb*, planted by John Nash
Top right - Red Campion, Cow Parsely and Mares' Tales
Bottom - Fallen willow, (Helen Harrison)

Window at Bottengoms, 1984, Glyn Morgan

SIDO, COLETTE AND ALISON UTTLEY

One can only be selective. As the sap rises, the ink flows. So it has ever been. The writer, penned up in his stuffy room all winter, feels himself as let out in the spring as the beasts, and naturally it is the garden which first catches his eye. There is much to put down. Never mind if it has all been said a thousand times before and a thousand springs ago. The writer doesn't care. Nature repeats its order and he repeats for the most part what generations of novelists, poets and stylish horticulturists have said on the subject. There are countless cultivated acres of spring-garden writing, most of it private, though open to view. The reader doesn't care. The same joyful clichés shoot up over the centuries and he himself would fill pages with them if only he had a moment to spare. 'Spring has returned,' wrote Rilke, 'and the earth is like a child that knows poems.'

This spring I return to two, never more contrasting, women whose gardening comment and philosophy have pleased me for years, Colette and Alison Uttley. I make them step forward from the multitude who dig and plant and tell, not because they are the best (no garden writer is this), but because each in her different way is so passionate – the only word – about spring flowers, spring air, spring's capriciousness. Their gardens are those of childhood, one at Castle Top Farm in Derbyshire, the other at Manor Farm in Saint-Sauveuren-Puisaye, Burgundy, and they carried them with them, so to speak, for the rest of their lives. Alison Uttley's garden is that of chilly early spring, Colette's of approaching summer heat – although she revels in a good unseasonal shock, such as snow on roses.

Spring-cleaning in the shape of billowing linen, and spring livestock, snap and cry just beyond their stone walls. These farm gardens are for intelligent ladies to rear clever daughters in. Colette's mother, the incomparable Sido, has one overriding word. It is 'Look!' Alison Uttley, the little girl who will become a scientist, never requires this injunction. Her rural essays are brilliant with minutiae accurately retrieved, and especially the minor details of old country gardens.

The spring gardener is at his most tolerant when it comes to

Spring Flowers,
wood engraving,
John Nash, 1935
Flowers and Faces

'wildings', as Alison Uttley calls them. When one comes to consider it, a lot of her garden writing is about finding the first coltsfoot, white violets and cowslips. 'These flowers, the wild flowers and the ordinary little garden blossoms, were part of our life. . . They were brave immortals, who were always beautiful . . . We felt we were immortals with them.' She says that few wildings were ever refused a home – except the dandelion, *dent de lion*, lion's tooth. It took me a long time to put up with having a fine dandelion in a flower-bed, making its space during spring and promising a great golden kingly head. During my childhood in Suffolk its double function as a diuretic and clock blinded me to its splendour, although I did have a faint sense of rapine when made to collect whole basketfuls of its blooms for wine. Alison Uttley is hopelessly indifferent to what ranks as a garden flower in springtime. In fact there isn't much gardening done in her books. Things just come up and are welcomed back. Like her, they stood the fearful Derbyshire cold ('The word "December" was like music to me'.) and in February, March and April she would receive them with a mixture of correct botany and frank lyricism. But, it being a farm, the kitchen garden was quite another matter. Although there flourished here 'a spectacular root of red cowslips, which my father had propagated himself from a cowslip root . . . There were no weeds, for somebody weeded it with great thoroughness, and it was not the children of the house.'

Colette, after walking home from school to Sido, on her knees in that lovely, holy garden described in *Earthly Paradise*, is not set to toil either. Children hate gardening, anyway. One has to give them one to make them work. Alison Uttley was given a space to make a rock garden, the object being to collect as many species of stone as plants. Aged ten my first garden was a rockery made on a mound beneath flowering greengage trees. It did not contain a single rock, it being Suffolk, only big flints which had been dragged out of the fields by the plough, and brick sunflowers and other entablature from an abandoned

Cottage garden,
Aston Upthorpe,
Berkshire, 1960s,
Edwin Smith

brickworks nearby. Seeds from penny packets of annuals were poured between their sharp edges in May after I had scraped all the fallen blossom from where I wanted to set them. My brother and I jealously guarded our brick and flint rockeries with half hoops of willow which would sprout in the spring. I don't know who told us about this kind of fencing but fresh graves in the churchyard would be willowed like this until they had settled. Colette's *Earthly Paradise* is urgent with instruction for the child in the garden. She wants everybody to hear her mother saying, 'Look!' A Burgundian farm garden is where both of them, who were always beautiful, who never grew old or grey, the exciting novelist to be, and the Parisian widow carried off to the country by the dashing Captain Colette, first fell in love with flowers.

In her garden my mother had a habit of addressing to the four cardinal points not only direct remarks and replies that sounded, when heard from our sitting room, like brief inspired soliloquies, but the actual manifestations of her courtesy, which generally took the form of plants and flowers. But in addition to these points – to Cebe and the rue des Vignes, to Mother Adolphe, and Maître de Fourolles – there was also a zone of collateral points, more distant and less defined, whose contact with us was by means of stifled sounds and signals. My childish pride and imagination saw our house as the central point of a mariner's chart of gardens, winds, and rays of light, no section of which lay quite beyond my mother's influence.

… 'I'm really very worried. I can't remember whether it was a family of crocus bulbs I planted there, or the chrysalis of an emperor moth.'

'We've only got to scratch to find out.'

A swift hand stopped mine. Why did no one ever model or paint or carve that hand of Sido's?

More garden looking goes on in the spring than at any other season. Some years ago I was in the Yonne in May and very close to where Sido

95

made her garden, and peering through lilac-locked gates like hers, while bells for the Ascension jangled from Vézèlay. In Essex the lawn-mowers would have been in full swing. My farm garden has few lawns as such, but many wide lawn paths, the widest alongside the orchard and cut against a swaying wilderness of blossom, cow parsley, buttercup and fritillary. On 21 April 1787 Gilbert White wrote, 'Mowed the grass-walks in part: they were crisp with hoar frost. Cut some grass in the orchard for the horses.' In May 1793 he was still being tidy. 'My

Auriculas,
wood engraving,
John Morley

weeding-woman swept-up on the grass-plot a bushel-basket [he is very fond of hyphens] of blossoms from the white apple-tree: and yet that tree seems still covered with bloom.' On Sunday, 19 April 1942 James Lees-Milne noted, 'Francis has been mowing the lawns round the house with the motor tractor, leaving the dead grass lying, so that there is a heavenly amber-sweet smell of hay, as in midsummer. I wish there were more wild flowers here besides the dandelions, which I love and others disdain. I lay on the grass and peered closely into the head of one. It was like looking into the inmost recesses of the sun, a swirl with petal flames alive and licking each other. To think that each of the million dandelions in Buckinghamshire, which are taken for granted or ignored, is in fact a marvellous star of golden beauty. How blind human beings are to the best around them . . .' In May 1918 Virginia Woolf was with her sister at Charleston: 'I lay with my window open listening to a nightingale, which beginning in the distance came very near the garden. Fishes splashed in the pond. May in England is all they say – so teeming, amorous, and creative.'

Geoffrey Grigson grew very pessimistic when it came to our national response to the passionate nature of the seasons.

I think in England we came somewhere near such seasonable observances as moon-viewing or viewing orchards in flower, such a classification, a ritualization, of sensual enjoyment, a hundred and twenty years ago, in the wake of our romanticism, only then it was too late.

Is it? I don't myself believe so. But should you, this spring, have been too active to have seen and absorbed what has happened in your garden, then obey Sido. Look closely at what usually escapes your glance. Let it engage each sense.

Wild Marjoram,
Peter Moyse

A GAMEY KIND OF PLANT

No more than a patch of *Fritillaria meleagris*, i.e. guinea-fowl, ever grows beneath the woody old laburnum, although it may have had its beginning under shrubs and not in damp pastures. But there it is every May, a few speckled or paper-white bells with a pile of either sombre or recreational associations. The poet Gerard Manley Hopkins described them as 'Snake's heads like drops of blood', and the Elizabethans as the 'Drooping Bell of Sodom'. I prefer to see them as namesakes of the dice-box, *Fritillus,* which every Roman soldier carried in his pack. Once when the fritillaries bloomed a curious box containing six Roman nails arrived, half a dozen of all sizes from the vast nail find near Perth when archaeologists excavated a hurriedly abandoned fort as Agricola's army was urgently required elsewhere. It was between 87-90AD. Such nails would have been hammered through the hands of Christ. I placed them by the dice-box flowers and saw twenty centuries of faith rush back to its roots. A routine execution and the rattle for the robe. The shaking hands and the pierced hands. However, John Gerard's *Herbal* prefers chess to dice. He likens fritillaries to 'the table or boord upon which men plaie at chess, which square checkers the flower doth very much resemble!'

Years ago when I lived in Debach I would cycle to Framsden to see Queenie Fox's famous fritillary meadow. It was about eight miles from my small farmhouse. Framsden was where I saw Hickey, the fancy dancer in *Akenfield*, take the floor and where I sat in the churchyard to write it down. He was a dandy, though gloomy, and had I asked I expect he would have

Fritillaria, Charles Rennie Mackintosh, Walberswick, 1915

called Queenie's fritillaries something like Lazarus's Bell. In the Thames Valley they were known as Frawcups and had their own festival. There could have been few in Framsden this past century and a half who would not have known where the snake's heads grew.

The fritillary meadow was about two acres of damp rich grass with a lush, reedy drainage ditch running the length of it. For fifty weeks of the year it was just another strip of pasture. But in late April it was metamorphosized as if Persephone had walked through it. The fritillaries rose in their thousands, a few of them dead white but the majority of them the muted purple colour with its reptilian markings which had given them their nickname. The effect was at first more strange than lovely in Suffolk eyes. I walked through the stackyard of Boundary Farm and down a cattle track expecting at my first visit to see something akin to the excitement of a bluebell wood. Mr Fox stood at the gate, hosting his guests and a young policeman guided three cars to the parking place, for the fritillaries were not as yet famous. At the bottom of the field stood Queenie, tall, elderly and smiling. For a few spring Sundays her meadow had become her front room. There were nightingales, and a chilly wind blew, and I imagined the flowers rustling as they swayed. We were welcomed into the field, not asked to walk round it. Dotted here and there among the blooms were other guests awkwardly striving not to tread on them. Almost immobilised by the flowers at our feet, we became trapped like figures in the floral margin of a book of hours. Queenie had no such qualms. She strode around picking handfuls of both purple and white fritillaries to press on us. It was what all country people did when their relations and friends visited their gardens. You couldn't leave without a generous bunch of sweet williams in particular.

I put mine in the bicycle bag and worried about them. Already, like shot birds whose feathers quickly dull, they were looking less glorious than before Queenie and myself had got our hands on them. And I still feel a pity for the mountain of cut flowers which nowadays adorn churches, brides, funerals etc. Fritillaries are not rare, if not as plentiful as they were. Unlike bluebells, they do not crowd each other but space themselves out in the wet new grasses, the purple ones darkly, the white ones with a certain mystery. I would re-plant those under the laburnum to where they could better spread themselves but this spot has so long been their hereditary home that I hesitate to uproot them from it. They tell me, 'We may not make much of a show like Framsden, but each spring do we not give you pause?'

FLORA BRITANNICA ARRIVES

Richard Mabey arrives and lays *Flora Britannica* on the dining-table. It is monumental. The half had not been told me on our walks. It is grand and beautiful, even breathtaking. We look at each other with a big shared happiness. The sheer organisation of it takes my breath away. Why isn't he gaunt and as thin as a rake, or like Shakespeare after his scribbled 'The wonder it hath endur'd so long' on the last page of King Lear. But no. He is the old walking, eating Richard and soon we shall ramble off to do both. It will not be until he has driven home to the Chilterns that I will for the first time open *Flora Britannica* to see his eye and hand everywhere.

There are a great many ways of holding on to our sanity amidst the vices and follies of the world, though none better than to walk knowledgeably among our native plants. And here is a text which allows the ordinary commonsensical flower-watcher to make common ground with the botanist proper. Richard has amalgamated science and lore, expertise and native anecdote, and so his book joins those of Geoffrey Grigson and William Keble Martin, John Gerard and John Clare as each age counts and explains its flowers. His mandate was to make connections between what was understood about plants before and after Linnaeus, before and after modern medicine, before and after religion's notion of them. Where the latter is concerned he is saying what Christ said, 'Consider the lilies'. Here are considerations which halt the gaze, which remind me if ever I need be reminded that Britain is marvellously floral still, its gloom-sowers notwithstanding, its chemicalisers do what they will. I see the tenacity of many a hard-hit specimen. Their come back strength. And I am reminded of Mrs Smith in Hardy's *A Pair of Blue Eyes* who deplored the kind of flower 'which neglect won't kill'.

I once took Richard to St Juliet when I was helping to edit the New Wessex edition of Thomas Hardy's works and we climbed around the

Meadow Saffron,
wood engraving,
John Nash, 1927

Greater Plantain,
Mattioli's *Herbal*,
1562

wild flower stone hedges of Cornwall before seeing the Padstow 'Oss do its strangely heartbreaking dance through the May Day streets. Such spring flowers, such re-sprung landscapes, such roaring seas. Such warm doorsteps to rest on as the procession passed and repassed, such bursting pubs. The *Flora Britannica* would have been seeding in his head. Thrift for example, with its 'hazy pink flowers' cushioning the cliffs. I had been enchanted by thrift ever since I was twenty and sat on the then un-built-over Lands End, mesmerised by its scented pressure on my bare feet and the great hulking waves breaking far below. Cornwall. Thinking again of Mrs Smith's defiant flowers and their deathlessness, I turn to Richard's descriptions of old hay meadows with their cut and come again blooms. Trees too do well with drastic management. What should be their scars become handsome evidence of their utility. Few if any of our contemporary naturalists possess Richard's ability to unify scientific and popular understanding of plants. The excellence of his *Flora Britannica* has much to do with the writing itself. Facts are one thing. His factual prose quite another.

Also he manages to include in his writing the joyousness which is a feature of our walks, the freshness with which he sees everything. Although it is piled high with contributors it remains his private flower atlas through which he leads the reader as if on a journey which they too have travelled now and then, but missing things all the way. Encyclopaedic writing demands our gratitude, nothing more. But Richard's is pretty amazing. He had indexed his heart-beats.

Meadowsweet, *Filipendula ulmaria*. In July the frothy white flowers of meadowsweet spill out of damp ditches and across riverside meadows throughout Britain: 'Sweet Green Tavern is a pub in the heart of Bolton, on an island between two arterial roads near the railway station. In the eighteenth century the area was the site of "Sweet Green House", so called because of the meadowsweet that grew prolifically all around.' Meadowsweet may have been named initially because it was used to flavour mead, the drink, not because of its adornment of meads and meadows. But vernacular names will always broaden if there is an opportunity for them to absorb new layers of meaning . . .

For the old layers of meaning Richard has gone to a vast number of correspondents up and down the land, and from them gathered fanciful tales and great truths, an enchanted language and a seemingly endless history of what grows, and making a kind of Domesday of flowers. It includes the utilisation of plants as cures and flavourings, and as just solid food. Here is the sickroom larder and the healthy menu.

But the essence of this fat book is that 'consider the lilies' injunction, that command to *think* about what grows in these islands, to understand it, if only via a legend. Human beings have a way of extending their

Hawthorn leaves and fruit,
The Chapter House,
Southwell Minster,
from *Flora Britannica*

parochialism to flowers and trees, acknowledging a shared soil and climate. They would find their way about via 'where the white violets grow' or the 'old cress ditch' and in particular via some local specimen of tree – in his case a Chilterns' beech of course. Although often we have not been there before. To the Scottish cotton thistle said to have been planted at Fotheringay in memory of Mary, Queen of Scots, for example, and still blooming. Or those grasses which were especially planted to stuff church hassocks. Or the plant observance of children. Or the still unbroken pre- and post-Reformation names of many flowers, the salad leaves which the monks left behind and those flowers which spelled a future terror or bliss. There were plants for sex and love, and flowers which strewed the road to hell. And always – and among the most sympathetically dealt with – the flowers of the writer and painter and sculptor. The composer too. The harp from the Saxon ship at Sutton Hoo is made of maple.

ROBERT HERRICK'S ANNUALS

No other English poet has entered our consciousness as a lyricist in the current meaning of the word as has Robert Herrick. Though few have met him on the page, countless have listened to his distinctive voice in the concert hall. For every composer, it seems, has needed to set him. The list is telling; Arthur Sullivan, Gustav Holst, Roger Quilter, E. J. Moeran, Benjamin Britten, Richard Rodney Bennett, Arnold Bax, Elizabeth Maconchy, Peter Warlock, Paul Hindemith, Edmund Rubbra and many others have all gone to a little book called *Hesperides*. Its author, a London goldsmith's son, was born in 1591, the year when Shakespeare wrote *The Comedy of Errors*, which could have been a description of Herrick's life. Swinburne would declare him 'the greatest song-writer born of the English race' and who is to deny it?

But what of *Hesperides*, that composer-rifled book and what of its author? His name has only just been engraved on a window in Poets' Corner in Westminster Abbey along with that of Oscar Wilde and a few others who had to wait for national acclaim. We see it with satisfaction. Yet why, when we have learned to understand the world of John Donne, George Herbert and Andrew Marvell, have we tended to dismiss that of Robert Herrick as a not quite real world and have only been interested in it because it 'sings'?

Robert Herrick, engraving, Charles V. White

Any first reading of *Hesperides* is quite an experience. Knowing what we now know about human nature, the Church of England and the English countryside – although no longer the Latin authors – we find ourselves in a very strange land, a Christian-faerie-classical-botanical-Brueghelish Devonshire, and at once begin to take stock. Page one.

> I sing of brooks, of blossom, birds and bowers,
>
> of April, May, of June and July flowers;
>
> . . . I write of youth, of love, and have access
>
> By these, to sing of cleanly wantonness.

So there you have it, cleanly wantonness.

The scene is spiritual and at the same time erotic. As for the style in which this only faintly botanical poetry is written, it should be artificial, yet it is not. On the contrary, its conceit is an aspect of its realism. Herrick might have been thinking of singers centuries hence, only he was not, for Charles the First's musicians were setting them in what was to be a last performance of the old love-song before the new seriousness set in.

Hesperides was published in London in 1648. A more unpropitious moment in which to launch a volume of poems which reflected the zest, wit, amorousness and particularly the confidence of the Elizabethan golden age could hardly have been chosen. Herrick called it *Hesperides* because it came out of the west. The Hesperides were the nymphs who guarded Juno's wedding present to Jupiter, the golden apples. It was one of the labours of Hercules to procure these apples for the cruel king of Argos, which he did.

Herrick hoped that he had brought something to London to excite the public's taste for his notion of Devonshire. But after eighteen long years of exile there, and now a Royalist parson ejected like so many others from his living, he was to find that the boisterous, dazzling literary scene which had been his training ground as a poet quite vanished. Ben Jonson, its hard-drinking, ever talking monarch, was dead. His 'Tribe', those who had swarmed in his presence from alehouse to alehouse, the Dog, the Sun, the Triple Tun and especially the Mermaid, were scattered and silent. There was poetry still but it was different. It repudiated everything which Robert Herrick, now in his fifties and ancient according to the standards of his day, represented, tolerance, old joys and rituals, and an amorality which was lightly held in check by religion.

Hesperides certainly included some 'Noble Numbers' as Herrick entitled his religious verse which should have acted as a bait to the Puritan reader, but chiefly it was seen as a riot of poetry which all too freely brought to town the country scents of women and flowers in a shameless mixed bed, horticulturally speaking. Gardeners would find instructive

July, John Nash, *The BBC Book of the Countryside*, 1963

107

verses such as 'How Primroses came green', 'How Lilies came white', 'To a Bed of Tulips', etc. unhelpful. And the perfect 'Fair Daffodils, we weep to see/You haste away so soon' is far too sad for them. As for 'The Lawn' being like 'Julia's skin'! And what of Parson Herrick and this pretty friend worshipping, not in his parish church but in a garden folly?

> Besides us two, i' the Temple here's not one
> To make up now a congregation.
> Let's to the altar of perfumes now go,
> And say short prayers: and when we have done so,

Danewort,
Mattioli's *Herbal*, 1562

Then we shall see, how in a little space

Saints will come in to fill each pew and place.

The truth was, of course, that he was glad to be ejected.

Come, leave this loathed country life, and then

Grow up to be a Roman citizen . . .

And to the farm-house ne'er return at all;

Though granges do not love thee, cities shall.

Herrick was a poet who revelled in the pleasures which his nose provided, whether they stemmed from the gardens of Dean Prior, his little parish on the edge of Dartmoor, or whether they were those, mixed with musk, which country girls released as they unlaced. Here was a writer who could be either intimate or scathing about his rustic flock. Some of them were a rough lot, ignorant and awful, some of them caught his fancy. Such is an English village.

A now serious London would read about the burial of village children, that everyday event which Herrick raised to an exquisite form of mourning. Or it could follow him as he pursued a young couple which he had just married into the bridal chamber itself until they sank from his sight into one of the best feather-beds in poetry. How out of touch with the times he was, and dangerously so. If his *Hesperides* did not make him notorious, rather than famous, it was because it did not sell. Nor would it until the nineteenth century. New, it was thought old fashioned. When found in Tennyson's England it was as fresh and dewy as a summer's morning. The composers leapt on it.

The Herrricks had arrived in London from Leicester in the 1550s. They lived in what John Stow, the Ackroyd of his day, described as 'the most beautiful frame of fayre houses and shoppes' in the city. This was Goldsmiths' Row, Cheapside, a gilded, shining, ornate address which would continue to beckon Herrick in his unloved Devonshire. It was not because of the family business. He had run away from this as fast as he could. It was because 'Golden Cheapside' harboured the last of the Titans, Ben Jonson. So although he had escaped to Cambridge, his true university was in the various taverns where Jonson held court. Later, he would be frugal with the facts of his London life. He confesses to having had a 'wild time' there but offers no details. But it was there that he began the practice of covering his tracks with his 'Silvers' and 'Julias'. In Dean Prior one would have imagined him a Roman Catholic celibate who was covering his tracks, not an Anglican parson. Why did he not wed? Why no wife for him when the matings of the local boys and girls were more of a shared joy than some wistful longing? What he did, of course, was to plant them out in his vicarage garden.

GALLIVM

Unfer frawen wegstro.

Lady's Bedstraw,
Fuchs' *Herbal*, 1542

The least hidden of Herrick's confessions are those which describe his drunkenness. How the Devon ales and the cowslip wine went round! It makes one's head split to read about it. A sagacious critic saw in his work 'a deliberate, though mild, *indecorum* of imagery, such as when Julia's leg is praised for being "as white and hairless as an egg"', and said how this 'helps to create a kind of pastoral effect even in poems in which there is no overt reference to country life'. Well said. Robert Herrick makes the English pastoral unsafe. We believe that we tread on trustworthy rural ground, with girls on loan from the classical authors, only to find ourselves in sexy landscapes. Indoors there is the poet's maid Prue, out of doors there are the desirable lovers. Yet all is a place of exile.

A popular notion of Herrick used to be that of a townee like Virgil who had been banished to live in what the Reverend Sydney Smith was to call 'a kind of healthy grave', i.e. the countryside. But this was to ignore what towns were like in the seventeenth century, and London famously so, streets backing on to hedges, fields, orchards and gardens, and a river which in summer was full of youthful bathers. Thus Dean Prior sometimes lacked for him country pleasures. When he was ejected from his living and made the huge five-day journey back to Westminster, with forty years poetry in his baggage, he said that he would rather die than have to return to Devonshire. But in 1660 the King came home and Herrick was restored to his rustic parish. He 'went abroad' to it, as he was legally obliged to do so, and he stayed in it until his death at eighty-four. They buried him in an earth which was part patch of Elizabethan literature and part patch of Horace's *Eclogues*, and part patch of a country world which he had invented, no one knows why or how.

> Julia, when thy Herrick dies,
> Close thou up thy poet's eyes;
> And his last breath. Let it be
> Taken in by none but thee.

And all the composers cried, 'At last, at last! Such perfect non-horticultural garden words for us to set to our music!' as they scrawled their bars.

SUMMER SOUNDS

Gardens are for listening in as well as for looking at. I am reminded of this every early summer when long days are spent out of doors and when, in fact, the house becomes a minor accessory to what occurs in its setting. Even at night, with all the windows agape, the bed seems to be as much in the garden as in a room. It is chiefly because of garden sounds. They are especially luxurious then, the movements of small creatures, the cry of owls and the delicious rustling of leaves in the lightest of warm winds creating a wild kind of comfort. There are scufflings. Bluetits are nesting in a rotting window-frame and sparrows and starlings are bringing up irritable families under the tiles. Once I heard the cat snoring in the flowers below, and this after he had slept all day on hot flagstones. These night-time garden noises come wrapped in scent. I imagine I hear roses spilling to the earth – there are throughout the night the softest plops which are only a degree above silence itself.

The house is so remote that its garden would at first hearing appear free of all contemporary din. Then I realise that although there are aircraft, tractor and the vaguest of traffic hummings, I have learnt to edit them out, having convinced myself of having pocketed an acre or two of the old silence. But such tones are so low, so muted, that visitors don't hear them at all and often stand dumbstruck by what they call the peace. Now and then crackling Amy Johnson-ish planes fly over from an airstrip in the next village, often very unelevated and looking in. They remind me of childhood and the excitement of catching a glimpse of the flier's helmeted head, and of pictures in the *Rainbow* in which pilots always waved from aeroplanes cruising about in cobalt skies. And yet it is odd that total strangers should have these grandstand views of private gardens from a few hundred feet up. Should I write to the airstrip and request the names of these people who are always dropping in? Do they approve of the changes to the top lawn? More pertinently to these thoughts on garden sounds, have they any idea of how the brief advent of their machines raises the PND (perceived noise decibel) of my birdsong?

Birds certainly are a garden's main sound-makers. Edit them out, were it possible, and what noise remained would be uncanny. Due to the woodlands surrounding the garden, and beyond these the river with its water-meadows and contributory streams and springs, birdsong and flight sounds could not be more incessant or various. Once there were nightingales but now we do very well with the thrushes and blackbirds. Towards dusk the latter gives up its worried *tchink-tchink* and fills the darkening shrubs with exquisite fragments of music, the melody beginning strongly and then petering out.

Bottengoms,
pen and ink drawing,
David Gentleman, 1997

Garden seat,
Rousham, Oxfordshire,
Edwin Smith, 1966

This is when the geese from my neighbour's lake will whirr over in a rowdy, stately chevron, making for the river. Nightfall can be a moment of tumult. Later, I hesitate to walk near the orchard in case I panic roosting pheasants. Set one of them up, and half a dozen can crash from the trees in dreadful fear, overwhelming me with guilt.

A luxury – the work sounds of others. These are now rare. If there is a hoe clinking against flints it will be my own. But I have lain low and listened to 'the whistling scythe'. Andrew Marvell, who described it thus, wrote not only the quintessential garden happiness poem but also the mysterious *The Mower Against Gardens* in which Damon, a man of the natural or un-gardened countryside, inveighs against the distortions done to plants and grass by gardeners, and because of this the distortion done to the human spirit when it is imprisoned in gardens. The poet was then living as tutor to a young girl in a great house whose grounds, though lovely, kept the real world at bay. Reading Marvell, I often think of the distinctive summer sounds of keeping the grass down during the succeeding centuries. And not only that of lawns, but of the adjacent hay-meadows. There would be bouts of rhythmic swishing and the fall of green stems against the blade, followed by bouts of honing and the little screams of whetstone and steel. In *The Mower Against Gardens* Damon laments,

> 'Tis all enforced, the fountain and the grot,
> While the sweet fields do lie forgot . . .

But not by me. Although at summer out of sight and only here and there glimpsed between dense foliage, the sweet fields which island my garden contribute substantially to what I hear in it. The nearly full-grown wheat can sound like the sea. Grazing animals tear and gulp their food and faraway there are human voices shouting their side on, and bells ringing. And of course there is singing in the wires. This is usually the first thrilling sound which the isolated country child seizes upon, this and the relentless melancholy of collared doves. They were pleasantly gloomy then; now as I listen to them they are as much part of the garden as my own gasps of breath as I weed and dig. They used to say, 'leave', 'get out while you can', 'travel'. Now they say, 'You won't find anywhere better than this'.

The difficulty with what might be called pure garden sound is that it tends to disappear the minute I start trying to put it into words. But it is this sound of leaf and flower and bough being activated by weather which can make lying in the summer garden – or slaving in it – such a transcendental

Zonal Pelargonium,
John Nash,
The Saturday Book, 1957

business. Drug it may be, but it is one which I freely allow myself. I cut out the birds, the farm, the village, the drone and thrum of distant machines, even the noisy aeroplanes, on purpose to get high on the ceaseless whispering, pulsating susurration which John Keats came nearest to explaining. His disease kept him outside and all the Hampstead gardens became for him a kind of orchestrated air. In summer I breathe such air as self-indulgently as possible, not even pretending to read as I sprawl in the sun but allowing myself half an hour or so of the 'highest listening', or a tuning-in to a soft hubbub made up of the clattering of the poplars, the little waterfall, bees, the passage of a quite disconcerting number of small creatures, but most of all the thousand variations of plants encountering light winds. Meditation would be too grand a word for what I am up to. I am being idle and still and open to murmur and to bliss. Gardeners, like everybody else, should have times when they should stop doing, and just be. We all tend to forget that in making a garden we create a realm which has its own unique voice, and that this has to be heard. It is quite in order to fall asleep while hearing it, although preferably one should lie awake and consciously absorb what it is saying.

All I do is get the drift, from the line of oaks, from the tall nettles in the orchard, from my best roses, from the sky itself. Tom Stothard the artist used to make John Constable lie beneath tall trees on a summer's day and stare through the leaves at the segments of blue, and tell his friend, 'There you are, my dear Constable, it is all glazing, all glazing.' But Constable may have read Luke Howard's *The Climate of London*, a revolutionary little treatise on meteorology and saw – and heard – the meeting of vegetation and weather. It is not a silent encounter.

SUMMER ENDS

In David Gascoyne's 1936 *Journal*, the youthful English poet – he was then 19 – remarks how foreigners' impressions of his country are 'naturally strange, and only half recognisable, like a dream of a place one knows'. And he mentions the many descriptions of London by Dostoyevsky, Rimbaud, Verlaine, Strindberg, Doré, Van Gogh and especially Alain-Fournier, whose delight in Chiswick's flowery suburbs as a young man just before the First World War remains infectious.

Because of frequent literary encounters with the England of such visitors, I carry in my head a lively muddle of foreign reaction to our towns

Late Summer,
East Hagbourne,
Berkshire,
Edwin Smith

and countryside. Their response to Englishness tempers my own. One of the less conscious reasons why people travel is so that they can inform the natives of the lands through which they pass what they must not fail to see and hear in their own territory. Henry James was the best guide of all in this respect, the American who chose as his mantra 'Summer afternoon, summer afternoon'. English summer afternoon, of course.

This year there has been a long uninterrupted run of such afternoons. Too early for a London appointment, I wander off into Kensington Square, that jealously maintained paradise behind Barker's where the trees reach high in lessons of stillness and the creamy façades try to stay civilised, and not shout house prices at the passers-by. There are few of these and not one of them suitably dressed for the architecture, for the temperature this summer afternoon is 80 in the shade. If Mrs Patrick Campbell could emerge from her door or Talleyrand from his, they would step back into their cool halls with surprise. Bare sunburnt girls, old ladies in next to nothing and two gods in shorts with a van which says 'Drains unblocked without Excavation.' A pub begs its customers to leave quietly so as not to upset the residents. So into Young Street where Thackeray wrote *Vanity Fair*, borrowing his title from *Pilgrim's Progress*. This drift of connection takes me back to Mount Bures near Wormingford, where I live, on the previous Sunday when, immediately after Matins, in comes a majestic chap with a staff and a 'scallop shell of quiet' fixed to his haversack to tell me that he is walking to Compostella to honour St James.

Summer at Mount Bures, the 'mount' being the motte of a Norman castle and now covered in blackberries. It adjoins the church of St John the Baptist, separated only by all the village graves and a few yards of sward azure with harebells. It is high here, the church, the farm buildings and the brambly mount rising up together to form a complex which might be in Normandy. Behind a soaring hedge rests Mr Chaplin in his productive garden of Eden. Having jangled our church's two pre-Reformation bells, inscribed *Sancte Necolae Ora Pro Nobis* and *Sir*

Nomen Domini Benedictum respectively, and having sung four sweet Victorian hymns, he now has this summer Sunday to himself. He beckons to me and encourages me to walk through his runner-bean alleys and into his Michaelmas daisy forest, and even into his new summer-house where, being close on ninety, he intends to idle. He lifts up his eyes to the mount down whose sides he slid on mother's tin tea-tray, and the paths he weeded for a shilling a year 'when I was a boy'. I can smell Sunday dinner, and the empty commuter train rattles by in the matchless warmth.

Back at my home, Bottengoms Farm, I tread on fallen plums as I cross the orchard, releasing their heady rot. Angelic gliders, Chinese-white against the cobalt sky, ride the air currents, and the Suffolk woodland over the river smoulders with heat. As a youth Mr Chaplin worked the mill on this river – as did the Constables. John painted a picture which he called *Summer, Noon* but a friend called it *The Hay Wain*. To be pedantic, the vehicle in the water is a timber cart. But the picture is not about a wagon but that listlessness which arrives at a particular moment on a hot day when the very birds cannot summon up sufficient energy to sing a note and the landscape seems to go giddy and insist that nothing whatever must be done.

And now the summer, officially at any rate, is past. Gone. And I take out of its context my favourite acknowledgement of this fact, 'The harvest is passed, the summer is ended, and we are not saved'. The sad fall of these words has enchanted me since childhood. The editor of Jeremiah 8 from which they are taken has headed them 'The Prophet's inconsolable grief'. For what? For the ease with which people fall back into idolatry. What a great poet is Jeremiah! He thinks God should fertilise the fields with their bones; it is all they are fit for. The farm-historian, Arthur Young, witnessed something akin to this, the contents of London's charnels being taken to Hertfordshire in tumbrels and spread on the land as bone-meal.

Our village fields are already ploughed and tidy. They have turned from silvery stubble to black furrows in a week. No waiting, no hanging about, no aftermath or second coming of what had been cut. Not that anyone notices. No one looks at fields any more. Gardens yes, but not fields.

Many acres of them behind my farmhouse are straggling back into pasture and give a hint of the landscape to come. Our arable world stares nervously at the collapsed beef and sheep world, and realises that when agriculture takes one of its plunges there are no exceptions. The young farmers seem to have come to grandfather's worries. Who would have thought it? The young farmers come to harvest festival to read the lessons from the Book of Ruth and Christ's parables, and the biblical words sound less archaic than they did last year. The farming press itself is aghast in

October, John Nash
Benham's Calender, 1958

disbelief. Incomes halved, incomes fled, though not yet in East Anglia. Here the rented combines and rented ploughs have been returned to their owners, plus vast cheques for their use, and a rich quiet ensues. This latter suits me perfectly. I begin to lay out the autumn work and to walk far, sometimes towards the river, mostly nowhere in particular. Just taking this field-edge or that, or the old flight-paths on the American aerodrome and their peripheral service roads, and allowing words their head. For this is how writing is done.

Mountain Ash, Mattioli's *Herbal*, 1562

Autumn round here in the Stour valley is a kind of summer until November, when the river mists become chilling and soaking and all but the oak leaves sail down densely, and one is surprised into turning up the heating. But until this happens, the slow-motion senescence of the year permits a meal now and then in the October garden, and winter proper to be put out of our minds. The migrant birds clear off in no time and barn owls make themselves heard. The heart-stopping desolation of their cry cuts across our measurements of time and is the apotheosis of wildness. 'Sweet Suffolk Owl' sang Thomas Vautor:

Thy note, that forth so freely rolls,
With shrill command the mouse controls,
And sings a dirge for dying souls.

How creatures and plants unknowingly add to our Englishness – or our

Frenchness and the rest! My antennae are so finely tuned that I can smell England the second I emerge from a plane at Heathrow. If there is air like this just beyond customs, what can it be like at Wormingford, I ask myself. There the bedroom window is rarely shut against it and it enters with sun or snow, a national but non-patriotic air which is mysteriously scented with place and I suppose history, and certainly with everything which grows and hoots and wanders on this island.

It is the end of summer, the coming of autumn. The new season's falling, rotting and thus aromatic nature creates for me an essence to be found nowhere but in England. By all that is written about it, it should settle me down for the winter, but instead it brings me fully alive. I first smelled it kicking up leaves on the way to school, and still I breathe it in – my fix, my East Anglian stimulus.

POPE'S GARDEN AT TWICKENHAM

The present passion for gardening lures us to the creations of previous gardeners. Sometimes we find them, sometimes they have vanished. Sometimes they are in mint condition, to steal the bookseller's language, often they are time-worn and, like us, not what they were. Friends once traced the ghost of Elizabeth von Arnim's garden, now in Poland, and found her schloss gone but her beds and terraces still faintly present. The motives for making a garden interests us greatly, for there can be few works of art requiring more toil, maintenance and preoccupation. So why disrupt one's life in this way? The gardener's reply would be, 'In order to fulfil it'.

Why did Alexander Pope, the supreme poet of the eighteenth century and a financially successful one, immerse himself in a garden? So much so at times that the literary world of which he was so brilliant a part got lost in his horticulture for years on end. A few reasonable answers might include that he was an outsider by reason of religion and physical deformity, not to mention genius, which is itself isolating. Yet he did not belong to that group of gardeners who are accused by some of turning their backs on society and what is called 'reality'. Then there was his age. Pope was little more than a youth when he took to gardening, overturning the cliché that gardening was a desirable activity for the retired and an odd one for the young.

Pope's life was circumscribed by illness and mockery. Deformity or madness made one laugh in the eighteenth century. As for his faith, it was not much more than nominal Roman Catholicism – his father may have been converted during a trip to Lisbon. But it kept Alexander from the university. Virtually self-educated by his immense reading, he derived his early fascination with gardening, not from the fashionable practitioners of his time, but from discovering that the classical authors had a high regard for it. Another factor must have been his father's move from London, where he was a prosperous linen-draper, to Windsor Forest, then as now wonderfully sylvan, quiet and bird-filled. Peter Martin, garden historian of the Williamsburg Foundation in Virginia, and an authority on Pope's Twickenham, recognised what he calls the 'associative, the iconographic, and the emblematic' elements which played such a huge role in the poet's unique ability for his day form of garden-making.

Pope was both swept along by the magnificent Augustan landscape movement and resistant to its grandiosity. His was as private a garden as his quick-silver intelligence, family tenderness and learned understanding of nature could provide. Twickenham, though formal, was never the classics laid out on lawns. It was an expression of himself. He did not advertise it, or pose in it, as did so many of his contemporaries, yet when

Pope's Villa, Twickenham,
Detail from an engraving
by Rysbrack, 1735

he died aged sixty-four, his pretty Palladian villa by the Thames was renowned throughout the country. Too famous, too celebrated, alas, for Lady Howe, who purchased it some sixty years later. Hating those who came to see this garden which Pope had partly based on the garden of Alcinous in Homer, she destroyed it.

Pope's garden gave him entrée to the aristocracy. Eventually he saw this group as more of a spiritual entity which generated national values, rather than an upper class, and when both his greatness as a poet and his skill as a plantsman opened the Tory park gates to him, he became as much philosophically as socially at home. Those who had been on the Grand Tour used his translation of Homer as a manual for their gardening back home. Here is his sumptuous account of an orchard:

Close to the gates a spacious garden lies,

From storms defended, and inclement skies;

Four acres was th' allotted space of ground,

Fenced with a green enclosure all around.

Tall thriving trees confessed the fruitful mold;

The red'ing apple ripens here to gold,

Here the blue fig with luscious juice o'erflows,

With deeper red the full pomegranate glows,

The branch here bends beneath the weighty pear,

And verdant olives flourish round the year.

The balmy spirit of the western gale

External breathes on fruit untaught to fail:

Each dropping pear a following pear supplies,

On apples apples, fig on figs arise:

The same mild season gives the blooms to blow,

The buds to harden, and the fruits to grow.

The Odyssey, Book VII

Gardening rambles democratically over all levels in Britain. Gardeners, plantsmen, allotmenters, window-boxers, do not see themselves as some kind of commonwealth but they are. Alexander Pope actually worked beside the men who planted his trees. He told them, 'A tree is a nobler object than a prince in his coronation robes', updating or variegating Christ's remark about Solomon and a lily. Pope called Lord Bathurst and Lord Burlington his 'vegetable lords' on account of their love of gardening. When Twickenham was completed, he realised that he belonged to a world which was within a world, as do all gardeners. It was a gardener called John Caryll who steered him towards Twickenham when he was still a child. It was from Caryll that he learned that in a great garden, farming and romantic views, flowers and fruit, ponds and lakes, all had to come together.

Obelisk in Pope's garden
in memory of his mother,
watercolour,
J.C.Buckler, 1826

Robert Digby noticed this at Twickenham, so he would ask his host, 'How thrive your garden-plants? How look the trees? How spring the Broccoli and Fenochio? Hard names to spell! How did the poppies bloom? And how is the great room approved? What parties have you had of pleasure? What in the grotto? What upon the Thames?'

Alexander Pope's garden had to provide dreams, visions, food, amusement, and nourishment for the spirit and the flesh equally. He and Lord Bolingbroke, whose garden was simply called Dawley Farm, both wanted to see an England of 'swelling grain', 'loaded trees' and mountain-crowning woods. Prosperity in other words. The little poet with the crippled body and the fine eyes wandered through most of the new and lovely gardens of his day, and went on making his own until he died. Its pattern and scents continue to fill our heads and guide our thoughts although we do not realise it. Lady Howe may have uprooted his Twickenham but it goes on flowering.

MYRRH

In the Epiphany churchyard the talk turned to the disposal of sacred texts. The old priest confessed that he buried his – the Bible or prayer book which at last was coming to pieces in his hand. In the ground? How interesting. Better to mulch than to burn. Back home the word 'myrrh' brought my boyhood Bible to mind – made it rise in my head from some muddled shelf. Leather-bound, shaky, I saw that it had been pretty ancient when who ever it was had given it me. Anxiously, I turned to the back pages in case I had imagined their contents. These were revelations which followed Revelation, maps of the Holy Land, architectural plans for building the Temple and, best of all, my first botany. 'Myrrh', I read, 'a gum-resin produced by several species of *Commiphora* (*Balsamodendron*) and used to make perfume and incense.' In this Bible, aged twelve, I had written in a very loopy copperplate on the front flyleaf George Matheson's hymn 'O Love that wilt not let me go', 'I lay in dust life's glory dead' – I ask you. But bury this book? . . . How strange. Four-leafed clovers are its bookmarks. Which wise man gave the myrrh? Was he really thinking of the end of this boy's life or of scenting the birthplace? Are we allowed to speculate? As we know, at the end a city counsellor who was all too familiar with what crucifixion did to the poor flesh, took down the body of Jesus and bound it up in a hundred pounds of myrrh and aloes, the women assisting. It was from this aromatic centre that the glorious figure emerged in Piero della Francesca's 'Resurrection'.

My myrrh is sweet cicely, *Myrrhis odorata*, which smells of aniseed and grows in an ever broadening patch below the front door. It has frothy green leaves and perfectly white flowers. It is mythic, of course, and should flower on Old Christmas Eve, 5th January. But it is no more than a bundle of sticks on this date, dead and brittle. Gerard the herbalist recommended its boiled roots to old people who were 'dull and without courage', telling them that it would comfort their hearts. It used to grow in graveyards as a plant of memory and sweetness, says Geoffrey Grigson. And of course, by the time I had done my Bible botany and wandered through Asia Minor with Paul, and learnt to pronounce the names of the sons of Dan, Canon Hughes would be descending the pulpit and the choir would be rising for the offertory hymn. And in January the aisles would be faintly smelling of gas, not myrrh, but a holy smell nonetheless. I must check on George Matheson, he whose words I wrote on the fly-leaf but which have been deemed unsuitable for the *New English Hymnal.* He was an importunate hymn-writer who ordered God to 'Gather us in' (the BBC Hymn book) and 'Make me a captive, Lord' (Common Praise). I read him again in my own hand and wonder why at twelve I should be resting my weary soul in God and giving him back my life more or less before I had had any, but 'there you are then!' As Cedric Morris used to say when he couldn't think of what should come next.

But Bibles and prayer books do accumulate in rarely visited corners. Here is mother's *Apocrypha* austerely signed A. G. Blythe and which contains the enchanting *Wisdom of Solomon*, and from which I like to think that the Magi got their brilliance. 'For the spirit of the Lord filleth the earth.' But the print! The next size down would fit a pinhead. I magnify it as I must all things this season.

OCTOBER

No one knows exactly the origin of Autumn, a word which resonates in Latin, Middle English and French, and says that nature, including us, comes to maturity and must consequently Fall, as the Americans put it. It is a season for drawing-up into one's nostrils, as one would the fleeting scent of certain flowers, or turned earth, or the sea when one suddenly arrives at it after a long drive. It reeks a little of decay, sadness, chilliness and smoke, but it is an acceptable reek, although not to all. D. H. Lawrence couldn't bear it. He told his friend John Middleton Murry, 'The autumn always gets me badly, as it breaks into colours. I want to go south, where there is no autumn, where the cold doesn't crouch over one like a snow-leopard waiting to pounce. The heart of the North is dead, and the fingers are corpse fingers'.

October always gets me into the study with far greater resolutions to make and keep than those I dream-up on New Year's day. It is when I start a new book. The cold is still a fair way off from pouncing, fair-weather visitors from London peter-out – 'You'll be glad that you have got your new central heating!' – and in spite of the evidence everywhere that the year is no longer youthful, I myself feel strangely energised. Windows are closed, gardens are tidied, jerseys are found, nights pull in – but work stretches out, comfortably and happily. The fields are enigmatic. It has been a critical year for farming and could go down in the history books as one of those climatics of rural change. But the countryside itself smiles its way through at Luke's little summer, usually a blissful October fortnight in East Anglia, and says that agriculture is just a surface thing, and not to worry. Below the shallow plough marks the flint is doing well and the water table of the Stour is as free-flowing as ever it was. Winter birds call and the skies promise gales. It is all curiously settling. What a lot I shall get done, I tell myself, tearing September off the calendar.

What *has* to be done in the autumn, house and garden-wise is another

October,
John Nash,
Almanack of Hope,
1944

matter. Bright leaves vanish to reveal huge tasks. Such as coppicing the hazels and reducing a barrier to a hedge, sawing logs, raking leafy sludge from the gutters and a score of similar jobs. Nice heavy labour which can run in tandem with chapter one. And then there is reading. October brings piles of books out. Often two or three are being read at the same time and lie open in every room, to be temptingly picked up in that leisurely fashion which October encourages. I pick apples and lay them out in the old larder with its always mildly damp brick floor and its retained odours, a mixture of onions, potatoes, saved jam-jars, wine, baskets, cobwebs, useless but not thrown out kitchen equipment, ladders, and probably a mouse. The apples must not touch. They glow.

Hawthorn,
Mattioli's *Herbal*,
1562

This larder comes into its own in October. It contains the month, holds it in its walls alongside the ghostly whiffs of past Octobers. Even in June it breathes October. I should turn it out, but it would not like it. But I will scrub its waving brick floor and bring up its greeny yellows and moist browns.

Few fogs nowadays. The Clean Air Act of half a century ago has dealt a blow at English literature. What pages and poems there were on those marvellously lethal and atmospheric autumns which rose from the ground and created a thrilling backdrop for murder and sickness. You knew where you were in a novelist's fog. But all gone, and crimes are now committed in November sunshine, the murkiness of life vanished apparently for ever. The unhealthiness of current fiction is a great loss. It is hard to whip-up autumn drama these clear days. Sudden patches of river mist is all one can expect, although where it lasts the water meadows with their invisible banks and trunkless trees still become Chinese in the old way.

On the farm the combine is tucked up in its den for another year. It reminds me of the Padstow 'Oss who's glimpse of the sun is even shorter, a beloved monster stumbling around the town for a few May hours. The stubble is ploughed in, the ditches show their water through the thinning plants, the birds sing a different tune, or perhaps it is the note of coldness in the air which makes it seem that they do. But that the year is running out of time and warmth is unquestionable. I find it satisfying that it should, that seasonally it is out of human control and heads towards winter. I find myself thinking of summer woods, the towering woodland of Glenlyon in Perthshire, where I walked in June, and Royce Wood at Helpston, where John Clare tracked his nightingale, and where I plunged about in the blackberry undergrowth in July, and of them now stripping themselves bare. My own poplars languidly discard their leaves until they stand in black mulch and the westering sun which they blocked out all summer now blazes through their skeletons. Rabbits and hares, and even the fish under the bridge, have a homing look.

Quite where agriculture is heading for is this autumn's inescapable question. As the light shortens it dawns on farmers everywhere that the great rains and dreadful plague of the year 2001 have brought something to a head, which is that the kind of protection which has existed since the last war could soon vanish. Should this occur during the next decade or so, the countryside will not look either better or worse, but it will look different. And our view of it will be different. But the same old seasons will manage it, year in and year out, greening it, reducing it to sticks and stones when the North wind blows. Autumn makes for pensiveness. After Michaelmas the old farmers would tot-up the takings and would, every few generations, have to count on some drastic change, for agriculture, like every trade, has had to take leaps into the unknown. This autumn it will begin to think about where it has to go. And my farm garden will rest.

Eryngyum giganteum,
'Miss Wilmott's Ghost',
Bottengoms

WHEN THE LEAVES COME DOWN

My old friend John Nash enjoyed a dead tree. There are always one or two in the garden, often hedgerow elms which show lots of life for about twenty feet, then peter out. Huge old willows depart slowly, creaking and cracking and throwing their limbs about. In winter the dozen vast oaks planted along the parish border by a Georgian farmer are unable to hide the wounds of the 1987 gale and look half dead, though in leaf all mortality is concealed and, with their roots in a stream, they become magnificently alive. John's landscapes like to put in a little bareness in summer, a bony white branch here and there, a great slain trunk upright on the horizon, a stark poplar in July.

One day I took him to Staverton Thicks, Suffolk's instance of tree mortality, and more Arthur than Oliver Rackham. This ancient scrap of forest is enclosed by Forestry Commission conifers whose towering strength it challenges with its long and stately dying. John was silenced by this grand decrepitude. It was a place which bred silence and told one little. Its chief information where I was concerned was that Charles Brandon, Duke of Suffolk and his wife, Henry VIII's sister, had picnicked here. Its less reliable history made it one of the sites of St Edmund's martyrdom. John Nash was only peripherally interested in such events. What he now gloried in was the majesty of dead and dying trees. Not the brief rise and fall of the hedgerow elms or the tumbling sticks from otherwise far from perishing oaks, but the huge kindness of what now spread, or tottered, before him, an entire woodland population holding each other up. He stuck his portable stool in the dense mulch, opened his sketchbook and began to draw.

Staverton Thicks lies midway between the Deben and the Alde, and just outside Orford. Not far away is Rendlesham, the palace of the kings who lie buried at Sutton Hoo, and Havergate the avocet island. The sandy soils all around are humpy with tumuli and busy with rabbits. There is no birdsong in the Thicks, though pheasants sometimes screech. Yet the immediate feeling of desolation and morbidity began to creep away as John worked and I explored. Immense age and determined sap had between them created a strange vitality, a kind of tree courage which was grandly sculptural as holly propped up oak and oak holly. Hollow boles somehow produced sufficient nutriment to feed a budding branch. What kept such woods alive, if one can call it that, was this actual long-settled seclusion and climate. Peripheral barriers of guelder-rose and hazel kept out the severe wind. There was a close canopy of branches which checked excessive leaf. What caused this wood to exist? Long life or a long dying? Could it ever die? Its chief enemies were parasitic fungi, canker caused by sun burns through lack of shade, frost ditto, aphids, bark beetles, man – and lightning. They say that lightning strikes the oak more than any other tree. Cycling back to Debach from Framlingham I saw a great oak in the middle of a field blazing like a torch or an immense sparkler letting off its own thunder. When the rain fell, not daring to shelter under a tree, I stood in a ditch and wisely distant from my shining bike, literally wet to the skin and yet somehow exhilarated and 'elemental'. I now imagined Staverton in a great storm and taking refuge in one of its room-sized boles. But it was a still afternoon with now and then a brief cold wind from the North Sea, and the smoke from John's cigarette barely wavering.

I shifted about. A carpet-soft humus deadened each step. There were a few flowers, sanicle shoots, speedwell, wild strawberry. A series of glades offered variations of senescence, astonishing partnerships

Honeysuckle, John Nash

Staverton Thicks,
John Nash, 1956,
Aldeburgh Festival
programme

between holly, oak and ivy as they did all that they could to prevent each other's fall. Should I sight the boundary ditch or the fairy-tale-like cottage where an author lived, I would wind myself back into the cracking interior. Both my neighbours at Tiger Hill and myself possess woodland gardens where it is politic to let certain fallen things lie. But now and then I have a little tidy-up and make some log piles. My trees are full of birds, though no nightingales now. One of them was brought down by – a honeysuckle.

FINE FRUITS

It is not often that I wonder what they are thinking, they the distinct three small congregations of the three disparate churches, as I emerge from the vestry Sunday by Sunday. Year after year they rise and wait. Nobody says, 'We have heard it all before'. Should I ask myself what I am doing my true answer would be, 'setting a climate for prayer'. There will be some bookish instruction and a few seasonal notes, 'We will sing Benedicite instead of Te Deum because the spring, as well as Lent, is upon us'. As this is on the last page of some prayer books there is much fluttering. But how appreciative it is, this holy natural history. 'Do we have to sing it all?' By all means. The prayerful hour passes with little originality yet often something beautiful happens, though hard to put a name to. Usually the sermon, call it this, has

Wood engraving,
Clifford Harper,
England in Particular, 2006

been a brief literary lecture. Poetry and scraps of local history have wound through a collect maybe. Most of the hearers are old, old friends. And thus I imagine it has ever been, the familiar figure, voice, movement, the hug at the door, the platitudes which contain the concern.

This week I watched Desmond Tutu on television and in case anyone should have missed it, he told this joke. A plane was rocking about in the sky and the terrified passengers shouted, 'Do something religious' to a priest. So he began to take the collection. I once met this joyful archbishop. It was after a lecture at Essex University in which his happiness could not be contained in one lecture-room but had to be devolved on screens all over the building. It too, as much danced as spoken, set a climate for prayer. Quite what prayer it is hard to say. George Herbert famously left us with an exuberant choice of definitions, each one of them dodging the simple answer where he was concerned. 'Talking to Christ'. This was the most natural conversation he knew of. Access to it often unnerved him. It was like a poor man having the ear of his sovereign so he would interrupt his flow with, to this Lord, superfluous apologies. But as we know to our delight, Herbert was heard out. The Wormingford worshippers are heard out. The united benefice is heard out. I am heard out. Especially when we are not doing anything self-consciously religious but are half-dreaming through the Benedicite – or the notices, if it comes to that.

I have been calling-in the raspberries to their ancestral bed. Given a chance, raspberries will go AWOL. For years I have allowed a few canes here and there to fruit in flower-beds, a hedge, an enormous clump of *Hypericum*, amongst the spuds. But no more. Home they are and just in time for a nice rain. I transplanted them until a lop-sided moon feebly lit the river mist and the white cat rose from a wall and retired to the warm bathroom, her current couch. There were no raspberry prayers so far as I can remember but their earth was surprisingly soggy between my toes. Garden clothes go from old to useless but I won't preach on that. Dear old shoes, you who climbed the Cairngorms and trod the shores of Norfolk, who stepped through Sydney and into endless woods, you have come to grief in a raspberry patch. A lesson here, no doubt, but the oven has to be switched on.

*   *   *

The arrival of autumn offers a choice. As someone said, 'It can be a season of maturity, or of incipient decay'. Personally, I love it. In East Anglia it gives us some of our best weather. Those little summers of Luke and Martin have a way of outgrowing their calendar limits, so much so that when winter can no longer tolerate these dream days and bursts upon us we are in deep shock. But for winter to arrive, summer had to depart, and this is indeed quite sad. Poets harp on it.

> Nature now spreads around in dreary hue
> A pall to cover all that summer knew,

writes John Clare. 'Come, come!' I say. Where is that accurate gaze? But I will allow for some melancholy, some regret.

My head full of incomprehensible figures after listening to the collapse of Northern Rock, I walk to the village shop to fetch the necessities of life, bread, cheese and Whiskas. And run into Mrs Burge feeding birds, notwithstanding all the hedges bursting with berries. We exchange economic information. She says that she can recall when you did not get an egg in hospital unless your mother brought you one with your name written on it. In pencil. Mr Burge is out gleaning the onions which have tumbled from Mr Rix's lorries, being given permission to do this. He will bring me as usual two long strings of them, red and white onions, and hang them on the brick posts near the stream to dry out. After which they will dangle from the larder beam and feed me for the coming year.

Behind the farmhouse a twenty-foot wall of Traveller's Joy mounts the holly hedge, and pheasants and baby rabbits scuttle about in the orchard. I visit the horizontal pear-tree. From once fruiting at a dizzy height, it now offers its Warden pears a yard above the ground. I have never found out what

Red Antwerp Raspberry,
William Hooker, 1818

brought it so conveniently low. They are baking pears which I cook whole in a little sugar and wine and spice, and are said to have originated at the Cistercian monastery at Warden, Bedfordshire. They are devoured in *The Ingloldsby Legends*:

> The Canon sighed, but rousing cried, 'I answer to thy call,
> And a Warden pie's a dainty dish to mortify withal . . .'

Pear-pie. I just chop mine in half, stick it with cloves, splash it with left over red wine. sprinkle it with sugar, and put it in the oven. Nothing flashy. But the pinkness when it is cooked, the flushed skin, the sense of occasion! Food for autumn. From the fields there comes a bit of the old clatter and I open the window to hear it better, a many-toothed harrow rattling up and down, and Duncan shouting a greeting to someone, dogs barking, children bumping down the track on small mountain-bikes, horses grouping for conversation under the oaks. Not that all this lasted much longer than a last summer-day. And all too soon the new farming silence and village emptiness returned. What has to be done in a field now takes a couple of hours. I pick a Portugal quince for the window-sill. It will scent the room.

*   *   *

Judging the children's handwriting competition at the Flower Show, I am required to ignore the decorative borders. And I have a vision of the Abbot

September,
John Nash,
Almanack of Hope,
1944

142

of Lindisfarne telling the monks in the Scriptorium, 'Cut out the fancy stuff, just stick to the text'. However, the winner of the handwriting has somehow integrated words and design, and receives first prize. Of course, none of the handwriting boys and girls are present, being confined to the current infant purdah. On the radio I hear that only one per cent of country children have picked a plum and eaten it.

What a year it has been for plums. A fairly frostless spring and a rain-fattening July has made the boughs bend with fruit. No visitor to Bottengoms Farm has been able to escape my Victorias. As for my greengages, too good to give away, they fill the preserves shelf in the larder. Wild plums of every hue stay ungathered in the village lanes, gorgeous food there for the taking. Only there are no takers. The children should be driven from their computer dens to pick them and have their first taste of them, something they will remember all their days. They could write 'My first Bullace'. No sooner have I typed this wondrous name than I am twelve again and gorging on wayside bullaces with a similar greed to that of a woman I saw on the train with a large bag of crisps, stuffing them into her mouth at high speed. 'You will get the belly-ache', warned an old aunt who saw me under the bullace tree. But I never did. Wild plums for wild country boys. All too soon, ripeness being all, the highest, unreachable bullaces would plump down into the autumn grass and the smell of their dissolution would hang in the air until Christmas. Should we devour cooked plums at home it was a kind of culinary playing for high stakes to swallow a stone so that those on the edge of the plate read, 'Tinker, Tailor, Rich Man' thrice over.

In a Tudor account of imported food 'the plumme called the Perdigwena' was brought to England. But it is the blackthorn which is ancestral maybe to 'all the luscious plums of the garden, including the greengage' – I am quoting my favourite plum man Geoffrey Grigson. He is mordant on the bullace. 'As better plums have been raised, the bullace has more and more been abandoned, clinging to orchard hedges, old gardens, undisturbed corners, naturalising itself in neglect.' There are people who do this, of course. You

Gansell's Bergamotte Pear,
William Hooker, 1816

find them here and there, strong and fruitful and purely indigenous to a scrap of landscape, its very spirit, so to speak. It could be some Hebridian isle – or Norfolk. Faintly tart, like wild fruit, and entirely 'belonging', to encounter them is a reminder of the old sharpness and sweetness of life. They can be as wry as sloes – as children we would offer one of these to our London cousins to watch their mouths dry up and try to spit. After such an experience it would take some time to persuade them to eat a damson. Ah, damsons. At tea we would say, 'Could you please pass the *dam*-son jam' until mother would say, 'Enough of that!'

Now I must go out and gather crab-apples from a spectacular tree and make jelly. It grows by the tumble-down farm wall and eventually lays an apple carpet below it. In spring its blossom is a kind of enchantment. In winter it rattles. But now, at this instant, it is fruit-yellow and prodigious.

SEASONS OF THOUGHTFULNESS

The year continues to be before itself, as we used to say. A vast stretch of sunshine brought on an early harvest and, with mostly everything cut by mid-August, autumn has arrived with less than ever of its old panache. Corn and barley, and indeed many summer-autumn bridging flowers, have by late September become a distant memory. Autumn proper looks like being well on its way out before decline and decay takes over the garden. So I shall have to wait an extra week or two to see how the high crippled limbs of my oaks have been getting on. Half wrenched off by the great gale, they look like hiding their ghastly shredded tendons beneath an even richer foliage than normal until getting on for Christmas. But in the strong westerlies of autumn I hear them, swinging dead and making little screams. Although they thought nothing of slaughtering a small wood to make a ship or a house, the demise of standing trees awed our ancestors. My oaks will soon shed boughs as well as leaves, and this will make me think.

The list of tasks 'to be done' is tackled with zest. The running-down of growth and of the light, perversely, is for me a stimulus. I work well when the days pull in. Besides, I love their smell, their subtle, musky, rotting, aromatic exhalation. Garden-wise, I have to check myself in not doing too much, in not hurrying things along. Let the botanical decay take its time, allow the leaves to blacken and the seed-heads to dry and rattle. An old friend would always point out that decomposition is part of the life of a plant. So I watch the garden pretending to die when all the time it is secretly limbering up for another summer. And then there is the untold delight, quite late in the year, of finding a patch of cyclamen in full bloom under a wispy thicket of brittle stalks and here and there the odd rose making a second coming. Birds' nests are exposed in the naked vine, which must not be pruned until the last minute before winter. I leave them, never quite knowing who comes back to where and what.

In the wilds I scythe the nettles with a new blade and an ancient haft, and wonder why I had endured a bent and notched cutting-edge for so long. The new one slides through the stinging forest, laying it flat. Very soon, a soft nettle lawn will appear. This aggravating plant stowed away with the corn-seed which the Pilgrim Fathers took to America, much to their wrath, and indeed was 'the first Plant taken notice of.' It likes to be where men have lived, and flourishes on such a scale in my band of woodland that I have long given up trying to cope with it, and let it rip. Since I set a lot of broad-leaf tree saplings to replace the elms a decade ago, my elderly farmer neighbour and I, well-protected, tread a circle of nettles to death round each young oak, chestnut and sycamore. I find the first few autumns of these young trees, their bright leaves whirling past, affecting, for it is the start of a deciduous ritual which will continue all through the next century and beyond. The hollow elm roots sprout a few green shoots which won't come to much. Badgers and foxes and rabbits have scraped sandy routes under them. Mixed with mown nettle there is the occasional whiff of animal, raw and uncompromising. I have to raise the scythe a fraction to miss the base of my red campion, a lovely, abundant plant which I allow to reside in the flower-beds as well as the thicket. In Suffolk they used to call it Poor Jane. In autumn it makes nice glossy hummocks on the cleared ground. It possessed randy connotations for the Elizabethans, although, as with the suggestive properties of so many of their flowers, one cannot think why. They certainly found gardens very merry in ways which escape us.

Autumn is most formally announced to me by the softly purple and ivory *Colchicum speciosum* which suddenly appear, naked and flawless, where all the surrounding plants are spotty with age. One clump has bloomed on clay for years, and as always I am baffled that anything so unprotectedly pink and white and gleaming should find no difficulty in being alive and immaculate there. *The* autumn flower when we were children was the Michaelmas Daisy, every kind of which bloomed in huge bushes in herbaceous borders and in cottage gardens, the latter protected by old lace curtains on frosty nights. On Monday mornings it was cut 'for teacher' and the path to school was like a moving Birnam wood of asters. Massed in

The Farmhouse Window
pen and ink for Crittalls,
John Nash, 1958

147

stone jars on the classroom sill, their stems grew sharply rank – to become an autumn stench of truly Proustian significance. Is it my fancy, but are there far fewer Michaelmas Daisies now? We had masses of an aster which, I recall, was in full flower in November, and also a gloriously tall, purplish-blue daisy which spread out against the decorated stonework in church on harvest festivals in a simple yet perfect manner. Michaelmas Daisies were not thought much of by the country people, but they 'came in handy' when everything else was 'going off'.

Autumn is the most contradictory of seasons. It has far more warmth and sunshine than is popularly allowed it, yet it is profoundly senescent. It is sweet-smelling of corruption and filled with departures. So why does it wake me up as it does? I begin fresh work, I look ahead, I welcome the touch of keenness in the air, I don't dread winter, although it is just ahead. After all, autumn is about the inescapability of winter. It is saying, 'get ready, watch out!' But it is also saying something sumptuous about maturity and natural decline and about humanity being in the same boat as the plants, an inevitability which, though regretful, is at the same time oddly comforting. And for me presumably invigorating, seeing as how I am braced up by these sad golden days. A fine new stove has arrived to burn gale-wood in. My eye begins to fall on certain books for dark evenings. I gather in succession blackberries, apples, pears and quinces, also some tart greenish-yellow grapes. I put the mower away after the last cut. I wait and wait for the final leaves to sail down before I have the big last clear-up. It was Flora Thompson who wrote about how the oaks kept one waiting in this respect – 'Laggard to come and laggard to go' – and eventually, as always, I have to have two leaf sweeps. Our autumns in East Anglia often conclude in violence. The poet John Clare described this exactly when he spoke of the benign climate of October being destroyed suddenly by running winds which are like 'spirits in their startling moods'. The garden which has been so hot so late – 'We are still having breakfast outside' – becomes in turn tempestuous, dank and chill. I am forced to remember that

I live in a river valley. Late autumn is very Chinese. There are patches of dag in the lanes and massed mist across the landscape generally, dissecting the trees and imposing a dripping silence. And in just a few weeks gaudiness gives way to colourlessness. As the year ends I make my little garden count of flowers 'still out', but soon give up because there are so many. Always a scrap of red campion, always a rose.

Strawberries,
wood engraving,
Yvonne Skargon,
Hortus No. 74

ONE AFTERNOON

Sprawling on the grass I smell fruit. Not plums, not the tottering crab, not late raspberries, just fruit. Curling in the sun are some fruit books from my shelves, F. A. Roach's glossy *Cultivated Fruits of Britain* and Stafford Whiteaker's *The Complete Strawberry*, and I hasten to push them into some shade. Fruit, if one includes wine, must rate as our most delicious food. It tastes best when eaten straight from the bough. Our old Aunt Agatha, when we were small boys, was strangely stingy about this and would poke about in the dank autumn grass with her stick for falls, rubbing a bruised apple on her skirt and offering it to us with a 'It might have a wasp so watch out!' We wondered what she did with the apples she picked, such baskets of them, and she all alone. An old gentleman neighbour would say, 'Pick one!' and scent, shape and texture were our's at the first sharp bite. No wonder that Eden, our first and rightful home, was an orchard, although Genesis doesn't mention apples. What it does mention is the Latin *Malum* which is the same name for evil or apple – or 'an unexpected misfortune'.

English kings planted fruit trees. Alfred copied the Emperor Charlemagne's order that crown lands should be well-planted with fruit trees and herbs. Long before the Norman conquest Saxon kings were imitating the Abbot of Ely and making fruit gardens. To produce – I am re-reading Roach now – superb fruit was the kind of achievement which contributed to a nobleman's magnificence. All through our climate changes, all through the warm Roman years and the little ice age of the Stuarts, through heat and cold and dreadful damps we took our annual apples, pears and plums for granted, were thrilled with our peaches, nectarines, apricots and peaches, our quinces, gooseberries, currants and raspberries, and worshipped our strawberries. Apparently we did not care greatly for figs, medlars, mulberries and at one time blackcurrants. Grapes tended to puzzle us, although Mr Roach's calm and de-mystifying approach to them dispels some of our English fears and fantasies. His tale of the medieval vineyards puts paid to many a superstition. Vintage was as important then as now. Greek wine was high on the list of a Roman banquet and you only got one glass of it. Or rather cup. There are

The Morello Cherry, William Hooker, 1818

150

Roman wine cups in the museum at Colchester and I think of the dark liquid and stained lips. The Roman soldiers there got a daily ration of sour wine. The largest orchard in the Domesday Book was at Bitesham, Berkshire. It was twelve acres. London and every town and city was full of little vineyards and orchards.

Fruit travelled so badly on our appalling roads that townsfolk grew their own and the cultivations of beautiful orchards were a civic must. Grand public buildings were surrounded with fruit trees. Some of the finest orchards were created by women, especially the wives of the Plantagenet monarchs, and Oliver Cromwell made the planting of orchards compulsory. James I planted the wrong kind of mulberry trees and got fruit but no silk. He ordered thousands of *Morus nigra* when he should have order *M. alba*.

My friend David Baker is my Apple-man. He and the great apple-man at Aldham, which is very near the D'arcy Spice country. I look for apples in Mr Roach's list. It says that our oldest apple is *Decio*, c.450 AD. As with our apples, our pears are vanishing. In 1888 there were thirteen varieties on the Royal Horticultural Society's commercial list, now a Williams' Bon Chrétien, a Conference or my Warden has to be searched for.

Cherries we know about, Polstead being just up the road. It was our cherry village and our murder village. It was where young Bill Corder killed Maria Marten. When I was a child the crime and the fruit were co-joined on the market stalls:

> Polstead cherries! Polstead cherries!
> Red as Maria Marten's blood!

The cherries hung in the trees along with bird-scarers and ancient lace curtains as nets. Young people wore them on their ears. A woman who seduced a lad was said to 'have taken his cherry'. Mr Roach is severe about the cherry state of things. Imports have played havoc with our once sensational cherry orchards and foreign cherries, like foreign apples, have no taste at all. That is, taste as the English know it, sharp, juicy, indescribably delicious, and never 'Golden Delicious' that lying apple.

My strawberry-bed has gone and is to be replaced. 'Doubtless God could have made a better berry', said Dr Butler, 'but doubtless God never did'. He was an Elizabethan who would only have eaten *Fragaria vesca*, the modest common strawberry of our woodlands and a mere sip of this fruit. What would Dr Butler have made of a Keen's Seedling? Like all of us supermarketers, Mr Roach rages in vain about the current preoccupation with fruit shapes and the indifference to fruit taste. A wobbly apple on whose skin a thrush has left its beak-mark, what a find! But then I was brought up on falls.

The Shropshire Damson
William Hooker, 1818

I go in to make tea, the white cat in my wake. *The Complete Strawberry* is hot to the touch. The old house smells of cake and roses. Waiting for the kettle to boil I read that strawberry most likely comes from 'straying berry' and not from the straw which protects it. The Tudors devoured them cautiously, believing them to be full of dangerous acids. They are in fact 90% water and vitamen C. The Georgians liked the Hautbois variety and 'Hotboys! Hotboys!' was heard in the streets. Jane Austen used them to upset her characters. To draw out their true character. The strawberry masters were Michael Keens, William Langham, Charles Hovey and the immortal Antoine Duchesne. And then there is Tiptree strawberry jam and, although not today, the classic outdoor, all-summer dish, strawberries and cream. Next year. However, Stafford Whiteaker thinks it a sin to add sugar and cream to this glorious fruit and thinks that nothing should approach it. Let it be just – a strawberry, faintly rough and then, who can find words to describe what happens when the teeth trap it? Enough. The white cat bites Whiskas.

THE IRIS MASTER
SIR CEDRIC MORRIS AT BENTON END

The notion that he changed somebody else's life would not have appealed to Cedric Morris, and he certainly cannot be said to have changed mine. Not in any full, re-directed sense, that is. Yet it would not be as it is now without him. Not quite. Our meeting not long after the war, myself very young and he entering upon the first of his various stages of a coherent, beautiful oldness, introduced a whole range of new attitudes and ideas to

Cedric Morris in his
studio at Benton End,
with *Irises* (1958),
Kurt Hutton

Wartime Garden, Cedric Morris, c. 1944, Benton End, Hadleigh

Iris Seedlings, 1943, Cedric Morris, Tate Gallery

Cedric Morris in his Garden, c. 1957, Glyn Morgan

Cedric Morris Irises, 2003, Glyn Morgan

my existence which gave it just the right amount of carelessness it needed in order to survive. But no actual advice or preaching, needless to add. Just an unapologetic display of hedonism and regular work which said: go and do thou likewise. Why not? Quite a lot of artists and writers in the Suffolk villages all around were saying much the same thing, but Cedric Morris, with his own beginnings rooted in an especially attractive wilfulness, said it most eloquently. When he died in February 1982, after a curious sliding tumble through his overcoat to the brick floor on which we met thirty years ago, I thought, now there must be a gap, a great vacancy, the shattering of the first circle. But no, and for the simple reason that when people are in their nineties, as Cedric was, they stop taking up the full human space. 'He's not all there!' the village boys used to shout at some persecuted creature of their own age, and for some months past it was plain to me that, although he was in his chair at dinner, or trotting down the back staircases at Benton End, or cutting into the talk with all the old amusement and relevance, vital aspects of Cedric had already wandered off on their own devices, leaving us just enough of his personality to trick us into thinking that he was still all here and could be for ever.

He knew differently. Last Christmas, when the first deep snow had fallen, he said to me, 'Do they touch your sleeve like this?' giving a little attention-drawing pluck to his jacket. Well, they don't, to be honest. Not yet. But if I manage to live to be ninety I dare say they will. Except for being almost blind – we said our names as we kissed him – and except for having to let his beard grow in a blossom-white fringe, he had altered hardly at all. When we pieced together the ancient photograph albums he had torn up, the images of his early self grinned through the rents, proving that time had only done the expected surface damage, nothing more. The long-lastingness of the incorrigible element in him was particularly obvious.

I was taken to Benton End for the first time by James Turner, a poet who had come to live on the Suffolk borders in order to write and grow mushrooms. I remember the day vividly. It marked not only the meeting with Cedric but also my first understanding of the nature of the local artists and writers, viewed as a group. First that it was not a coterie in the St Ives sense, second that it was linked together with much historic subtlety, so that one was forever discovering past inter-connections. In any case, James Turner's friendship with Cedric, like that of John Nash and many more, was based more on horticulture than art and literature, and after a brief taking stock of me, Cedric led us out into the celebrated brilliance of his 'iris week', and I was initiated into a realm of flowers, botanical and art students, earthy-fingered grandees and a great many giggly asides which I didn't quite get. He had just inherited his father's baronetcy and this seemed to add to the comedy. The gardeners wove their way round easels propped up in the long grass and the artists, of all ages, painted peering visitors and dense foliage in the exuberant Morris manner. The doors and window-frames of the ancient house glared Newlyn blue and there was a whiff of garlic and wine in the air from distant kitchens. The atmosphere was well out of this world so far as I had previously witnessed and tasted it. It was robust and coarse, and exquisite and tentative all at once. Rough and ready and fine mannered. Also faintly dangerous.

'Well,' asked James Turner, as we drove home, 'what did you think?'

I thought I had never seen anything like it, the big scrubbed table and the wooden platters, the cool ochre room crammed with lustre and bold oils of seabirds, formidable women fatiguing the salad and discussing plants, knowing youths, candlelight and marmalade cats (one of the women was Kathleen Hale), wine, a single electric bar fire sputtering before an eighteenth-century bread oven and an overall feeling of spartan grandeur. This last impression owed much to Lett, who had lived with Cedric since 1919, and who was also an artist. It was Lett who actually ran the school of art, complaining mightily, though always producing from a chaotic kitchen the most delicious food and drink. Nor did his contribution end there, for having placed it before us – their meals in the gaunt Suffolk bakehouse were curiously stately – he immediately took up his next role, that of story-teller. The tales were either scandalously about himself or floridly about their travels and encounters, and were designed to shock and inform. If his facts were often inexact, his gist was transparent. Occasionally Cedric would step in and straighten out some curly bit of tale without condemnation or fuss, or with one of his bouts of glee. Lett talked through a big wicked smile like the wolf-grandmother in Little Red Riding Hood. With his large frame and rearing, scarred bald dome, a legacy from the Western Front, and his mocking courtesy, he made no bones about dominating the scene. Much, much later, sitting with him during his last illness, at ease and fond of him, I tasted little surges of regret about my early self which, contrary to what was generally believed, was neither prim nor charmingly shy, but steely in that non-giving sense in which the young frequently are steely. But even then, as the pair of old friends

Benton End,
Hadleigh, Suffolk

complained their way out of a world which they had taken every

advantage of, and which they had greedily enjoyed, I still found difficulty in telling either one of them, and it should have been Cedric, how grateful I was that they had deflected me from too much safety.

It was inevitable that I should become the Benton End scribe, especially as Cedric's notion of written information was one wobbly line on a postcard, and Lett's was as following:

Cedric was born, of phenomenal vitality, on December 10th 1899. He was the eldest child of George Lockwood Morris of Sketty, Glamorgan (who, according to Burke, was descended from Owen Gwynedd, the last Prince of North Wales) . . . Bored and nonconformist in his father's household he made off to Canada. There he worked as a hired man on ranches in Ontario where the farmers seem rather to have taken advantage of his unusual energy and his naïf

Cedric Morris,
Benton End, 1948

ignorance of standard wages in the New World . . . Eighteen months later, he seems to have been studying singing at the Royal College of Music under Signor Vigetti, whose attempts at raising his light baritone to a tenor were unsuccessful. He determined to study painting in Paris.

. . . In Paris he industriously attended all the available croquis libre classes at the Académie la Grande Chaumière and Collarossi; Académie Moderne (under Othon Friesz, André Lhote and, later Fernand Léger); and was one of the first to enrol at the Académie Suédoise . . .

And so it goes on, through the gaudy Mediterranean travels, Cedric's membership of the London Group and of the Seven and Five (seven painters and five sculptors), his hand in founding the Welsh Contemporary Art Exhibitions between the wars, the settling down in Suffolk and the post-war plant-hunting, painting winter travels, which I also vividly remember, and finally Lett's attributing to his friend 'an unprecedented breadth of palette', whatever that might mean. But the herald-like proclamation with its emphatic Gallicisms is mentioned because it contrasted so completely with Cedric's own version of events, not in detail but in tone. The past was all a bit of a mumble to him. If you listened hard you might be lucky and catch a glimpse of it, but no sweep of scene and wilful goings-on, and heightened in French, as with Lett. The reason was simple. Cedric was a pagan who liked the sun on his back and the day's colours in his eyes, and the tastes and sights and sounds of Now. On a really beautiful afternoon at Benton End he could be seen lurking amidst the vast blooms he had brought to Suffolk from all over the world, virtually hugging the Now to him, his brown old face tilted a little skywards and his person defyingly, or helplessly elegant in the brown old clothes. A tour through the beds was learned and hilarious by turn, Cedric himself becoming quite convulsed by the habits of some plants and people. It was a curiously unoffending mix-up of sweetness and malice, a cocking a snook at conventions which had wilted long ago, due partly no doubt to earlier such naughty responses to them. Contrasting quite overwhelmingly with this merriment was a seriousness about art and humanity which had a way of pulling one up, of forcing one to be entirely truthful about what one said next. The passing in turn of brilliant specialist information (usually about botany), ideas on painting, escatology, wisdom, period camp and the most memorable individual-respecting tenderness created the kind of mercurial atmosphere which I – all of us – never quite got accustomed to. It was, of course, a perfectly unselfconscious bravura language belonging to the old bohemianism.

I was intrigued and entranced by Cedric's creature-like satisfaction with present time. It made his days so expansive that although he was visited to an alarming extent, an enormous amount of painting and gardening went on, apparently without interruption. When he was ninety he cursed God, whom he still took to be some ghastly Sunday misery from Glamorgan, for 'insulting' him with old age, but his sensuous basking in what pleasurable little treats each hour might provide continued to the last. Nobody has such a good time as a good-time puritan. Although so unlike him, I was drawn easily into his conspiracy of laughing judgements and solid work, although, alas, I was too much myself to achieve anything approaching his freedom.

He had exhibited regularly since the early twenties, with Lett and Gaudier-Brzeska in New York in 1926, with Ben and Winifred Nicholson, Christopher Wood (whom he taught), Ivon Hitchens, John Piper and the other members of the Seven and Five during the thirties, and both Wales and Suffolk had recently mounted retrospectives, but few artists could have done less to put their work on view. Seen standing amidst his landscapes, portraits ('not speaking but shrieking likenesses', as Raymond Mortimer called them), and flower pieces, the latter absolutely magnificent, a confrontation by vegetable hue and texture, shape and one almost adds scent which were nothing less than Cedric's notion of being alive in the world on a bright day, he acquired a quite awesome dimension which made even those of us who nursed white and ginger cats with him before the bar-fire hold back a bit. Standing beside him would be Millie Gomersall, his housekeeper for many years, ex-Fitzrovian and friend of the poet David Gascoyne during his pre-war Paris days, and herself restored to a kind of state by the unaccustomed finery which both she and Cedric had donned for the occasion. Although so countrified, Cedric retained much of the cosmopolitanism which Paris and Fitzrovia had given him. He perched in cities – 'When you took a room in Percy Street, you never asked for anything more than a table, a chair and a bed' – but luxuriated in an open landscape.

When the Tate Gallery celebrates him, it will be odd to stand amidst what will be the longest account of British post-Impressionism, as a single artist can give it, and not have it dominated by that rangy figure with its soft voice being so courteous and so improper by turn. Staring down at us will be, not only the company we shared at Benton End but the company before we existed, Anna Wickham, John Banting, Anthony Butts, Keidrich Rhys, Lucian Freud (his pupil), Rosamund Lehmann, Archie Gordon, Richard Chopping and Penelope Keith-faced women with names like Mrs Byng-Stamper. And the earthy Cedric geography of Umbria, Cornwall, Brittany, the Algarve, Mexico and Suffolk, none of it remote or exotic any longer, although in even the paintings of the sixties there is a quality which suggests that such areas of daily light and air and absorbing work take some getting to. Between the heads and the places will be the famous twenties birds, ravens, shags and herons, and everywhere his flowers, opulent, glorious, yet even at their most blazingly coloured and translucent, rooted in the soil which he had pressed around them. 'Not a boring thing,' was his ultimate accolade – rarely bestowed – when he was shown a friend's garden, and it was what he managed never to have in his life if he could help it, a boring thing.

The garden, Benton End

Yellow Flag (*Iris pseudacorus*),
Mattioli's *Herbal*, 1562

John Nash would say, 'Let's go and see the boys,' and we would go to
Benton End. Of course they would seem immensely old to me. I thought
at the time I would like to be an artist but they knew I was really a writer
and thought I would do a few writing chores for them.

Cedric and John Nash were old friends and fellow gardeners and would talk plants all the time. When Cedric came to Bottengoms John would say, 'What about artwork, old boy?' but then off they would go talking again about plants. Cedric always referred to himself as an artist-plantsman, which is what I put on his tombstone in Hadleigh cemetery. Cedric propagated irises in a shed in his garden. John disapproved of some of Cedric's iris species.

There were Iris Parties in June when hundreds of irises were in bloom inside the box hedges. Famous gardeners like Vita Sackville-West and other great plantsmen would turn up. David Horner who was life-long companion to Osbert Sitwell, used to come. He was a tall, effete figure. The young Beth Chatto was often present quietly absorbing this unique garden. I was a friend of hers, and of her brother Seeley. We would walk behind Cedric and John listening to risqué stories about plants – I learned a lot about plants and many other things. The conversation was racy and extraordinarily sophisticated. At 4.00 pm, Lucy Harwood, a neighbouring artist who acted as a sort of hostess to Cedric and Lett, rang a handbell to summon everyone for mugs of tea and rock cakes.

We all went to fancy dress parties at the house in Colchester of Dr Bob Sauvan-Smith and his friend Peggy Kirkaldy. Bob bought a number of Cedric's pictures and paid many visits. Among the artists who came were Joan Warburton (Maudie), one of Cedric's early pupils at Dedham, and Richard Chopping and Denis Wirth-Miller were part of the circle at this time. Nigel Scott, nicknamed 'The Bird', became Cedric's companion during the 1950s. He was a fine gardener and together they opened up the top garden at Benton End. He transformed Cedric's life in some ways but, tragically he died some years later while he and Cedric were plant-hunting in Madeira.

The tuition at Benton End was based rather on the Parisian atelier style – sitting at the feet of the master kind of thing. There were no formal lessons or lectures and students were encouraged to place their easels all over the garden. Cedric and Lett had lived in Newlyn after the first world war, and there was a feeling of Cornwall in the colour of the house and a definite whiff of the Mediterranean in the food and wine. The atmosphere was one of intellectual freedom. Everything was discussed. It was Bohemian in the best sense. Lett and Cedric were open about their homosexuality at a time when it was illegal to have such a relationship and they also conducted a fight against the philistinism of their day. The whole atmosphere was exciting and liberating.

Cedric had old-fashioned manners, was radical in his outlook and he didn't give a damn what people thought about him. He abhorred London and the art world. He was affectionate, unpretentious and never boring. The greatest crime at Benton End was to be boring! He had some close women friends but in general he didn't like women much and he used to say some dreadful things about them. He did nothing to promote his career – it was Lett who did that – but he knew his own worth. He was extremely disciplined in his working habits and toiled very hard at both his painting and his gardening. He didn't do a thing in the house and was oblivious to domestic practicalities. He never had much money. He never left the garden to walk down the High Street in Hadleigh – it was Lett who administered the school, did the shopping and cooking and the book-keeping. Lett was a good artist whose work was much influenced by Gaudier-Brzeska but his life was much taken up by running the Benton End household to the detriment of his work. The school closed in the winter when Cedric travelled in Europe and collected plants and Lett went 'for economy reasons' to Brown's Hotel in London!

I visited the house often and became loved and trusted by Cedric and Lett. They always thought of me as very young. The last time I saw Cedric I'd been to Sizewell beach with Glyn Morgan. We were both caught in torrential rain. I hung my jeans over the Aga, and Millie, the housekeeper, fetched me an ancient three-piece suit of Cedric's – which I wore to supper – without a shirt!

Cedric was blind at the end of his life and would lie in the sun like an old cat. His wonderful garden had turned into a hayfield with the exotics he had collected towering over the grass.

Cedric's work is beginning to be more seriously acknowledged now as truly original. He had a curious method of starting to paint from the top corner of the picture. He used an earthy but sumptuous palette. The lasting influence that Benton End had on me was a sense of openness, honesty and intellectual freedom. Not to give a damn!

*   *   *

Cusius, in his *Rarariorum Plantarum Historia*, 1601, confessed that 'a long experience has taught me that irises raised from seed vary in a wonderful way . . .' Just how wonderful he was four centuries too early to see. If Cedric Morris avoided most of the pitfalls open to the plant propagator it was because he was first and foremost an artist. His Benton End doubled as Art School and connoisseur garden, the two creativities

Cedric's grave in Hadleigh cemetery. Welsh slate headstone cut by Donald Simpson, flowers cut by Beth Chatto

becoming inseparable. Each sphere lent the other a singular authority. It was the painter as much as the gardener who gently transferred the pollen from anther to stigma, just as it was the botanist who made the canvases bloom with a kind of, at times, aggressive life-force. Watching him, I witnessed the moth-wing touch of omnipotence. John Nash flinched from the sight. Cedric's irises were certainly far larger than their lucent ancestors on the river bank, and the flags in the Hadleigh cottage gardens, but never better. He wandered through in his corduroy trousers and check shirt, his cravat passed through a silver ring, his skin like fine leather, his tall figure never entirely free of the youthful presence of his Paris days. He was a great laugher and he would reduce himself to tears, taking his pipe out of his mouth so as not to choke.

He had an understanding of plant mortality which affected his human portraits. An 'all flesh is grass' statement to accompany the vigour of vegetable and human life. 'Watch out', John Nash would say. Cedric would reach for a flower and look into it, his brown fingers, painty and nicotiny, their nails rimmed with soil, caressing its stem. With flowers, as with birds and men, he wanted them to give a truthful account of themselves. Petal colour was sensational, feathers warmed a breathing body. Near to his death, he said, 'Choose yourself a picture'. I chose one of the Algarve with washing blowing on a line in a backyard, and pear blossom out. The warm south. Too blind to sign it, Maggi Hambling wrote his name with a brush. Benton End was closing down.

Only Tony Venison, the genius garden editor of *Country Life* during most of the Benton End years, now knows what Cedric accomplished in his iris beds. My recollections float about in my head in a kind of Giverny haze. There were orchid-pink *Cordelia*, and *Strathmore*, the greatest pink iris in Britain, there was *Paprika*, a flower the colour of tarnished gun-metal, there was the ravishing *Fandango* which danced in the Suffolk winds, there was *Coronet*, a flaring near-gold bloom and some said the best yellow plicata iris in the world, there was *Susan*, all white and brown with exquisitely etched falls. There were *Beatrice, Abbot, Opal, Faustus, Apollo, Mocha* and the lilac-grey *Diane*, and many more. Many Benton End students were immortalised by a polleny paintbrush.

FURIOUS WINTER

I experienced my first winters in an East Anglian 'long house', one of those thatched, patched dwellings set up like wooden Meccano either in the village street or way out in the fields a few centuries ago. Father was lately back from Gallipoli, mother had lately arrived from Bloomsbury. They were very young. In winter the bitter Suffolk winds entered and excited this ancient building as they liked. Fires roared away on the hearth, inviting gales to join them. Water was drawn from a well in galvanised pails and I can still hear the silvery clinks of the chain. The pails were placed on a brick floor in the larder and froze overnight. The thatch dripped icicles and, in bed, we could hear small creatures burrowing-down for the night. Outside the snow was carved into shapely drifts and the trees cracked, sounding off chilly pistol shots. Neighbours swept a path to the garden gate and what vehicles there were turned the unswept road into a skating rink. But I was too little to remember the cold.

Bottengoms in winter,
Simon Dorrell,
The Countryman,
January 2001

Twenty years later I came to an identical long house in the Stour Valley, although this one had lost its thatch in Georgian days and boasted a lovely undulating pin-tiled roof which descended to five feet off the grass at the rear, known locally as a 'cat-slide'. The house had just been purchased by John Nash and his wife Christine. Like my birthplace a few miles west, it had no electricity and nothing 'on the mains'. Keeping the winter outside was a full-time occupation here, with the result that sometimes a Tudor fug was brewed inside. There were heavy velvet curtains at windows and doors, a coke stove like a grenade in the studio, Aladdin lamps everywhere, a blazing coal fire in the drawing-room, and plenty of cosy cigarette smoke wandering from ceiling to ceiling. Draft excluders (or sandbag bolsters) were placed where one might least fall over them. Hot cats were welcome to laps. We dressed up to go to bed, or at least the artists did, in fleecy pyjamas and bedsocks. The pin-tile roof got pushed about by weather and once, bringing John his morning tea, I found snow on his face. Breakfast

Wild Garden, Winter, (Bottengoms), watercolour, John Nash, 1959, Tate Gallery

had to keep out the cold, so we ate porridge, bacon and egg, marmalade and newly ground coffee. Getting out of bed in January was an heroic business, yet John ran a cold bath. I would listen to him hollering as he plunged in. In the studio Jack Frost had long been at work making enchanting pictures on the panes. There was anxiety about where I should write, where I might not die from cold. What sometimes worried me was all this carefully contained fug not sending me back to sleep. 'Don't let the warmth out!' was the cry should I open the front door. The back door could not be closed as it was stuck in a pile of house-martins' droppings. A second, interior door, massively bolstered and draped, kept us airless.

John Nash was the painter-poet-plantsman of winter. None knew better than he how snow fell on shell-holes and great gardens alike, the wrecked and the cultivated places. I would watch him as he contemplated the first fall.

Once we opened the front door only to be blocked by an enormous snow buttress and had to go out by the house-martins' entrance. Often I would be sent round the grounds to shake boughs which were on the point of breaking from their glittering blankets, and to catch the snow before it froze. John would draw from window to window, entranced by each vision, while his wife would call out, 'When Ronnie comes in, tell him the hod needs filling.' Winter in this old house was inspiring and, where keeping it in its proper place was concerned, a non-stop activity. Art and stories over, and a good tea laid (to be followed by a good dinner), John would play Schubert, the cats on the piano. The other day I found my copy of *Winterreise* – the words, that is, which were handed to us at the Jubilee Hall in Aldeburgh – and I reread them. They are by Wilhem Müller. The young lover is bewildered. In the spring his girl had mentioned love – and her mother, marriage! But for some inexplicable reason all now is coldness,

> Now the world is wretched,
> The path veiled in snow . . .
> Vainly I search the snow

For the footprint she left . . .
I long to kiss the ground,
Pierce both ice and snow
With my burning tears . . .

The programme note says, 'Please do not turn the page until the song is finished.' Who would? Winter is a kind of clearing-house for our desires and achievements.

About the same time as Schubert was composing *Winterreisse* John Clare was emerging as the master-voice of the English countryside. His life was part a winter journey in the madhouse and part the best and most accurate journey we have through the old rural experiences. These were fully seasonal, of course, and in a way in which they can never be seasonal again. For we have, except at certain moments such as the Great Gale, when they show their teeth, put ourselves beyond their power. Should winter hold up a commuter train there are questions in Parliament. Should someone fall in any icy street the lawyers are called in. Yet winter must be *lived* if one is to be alive to the annual birth and death of things. To reduce it to salt on the B-roads and filling up the oil tank won't do. One needs to taste its bitterness and see its cold parade. And, as John Crowe Ransom – a favourite of mine – said, to hear still

A cry of Absence, Absence in the heart
And in the wood the furious winter blowing.

It was the Tennessee writer Robert Drake who guided me to one of the finest of all winter poems, John Greenleaf Whittier's *Snowbound*. I read it when my farm track levels with snow and the normal silence of the house is 'turned up' and there is no getting out, and the telephone wires become swaying white ropes, and I count what is in the deep freeze, and listen to the aged settlement of beams – all this being a mere footnote to what occurred in Whittier's log cabin. While John Clare gives a series of fireside pictures in his 'Shepherd's Calendar', as with those Dutch painters, he drives his Northamptonshire neighbours out into the wild, wild weather. And here he is a master of wintry sounds, the clanking of pumps, the jarring of ice, the boy

> Shuffling thro the sinking snows
> Blowing his fingers as he goes

the plough horses 'Rubbing and lunging round the yard', 'the old hens scratting' and – masterly –

> Withering and keen the winter comes
> While comfort flyes to close shut rooms
> And sees the snow in feathers pass
> Winnowing by the window glass

Christmas Rose,
Bottengoms,
Charles Hall

– all of which I felt and saw as a village child but would have forgotten were it not for Clare. Winter is not unlike pain; hard to describe when it is no longer felt. Clare's feeling for it was that of a naturalist, a lover and an historian. It was also his reading time. Labouring in the fields during the rest of the year he would pray for rain, not for the crops but to send him home so that he could read. Winter was God's gift for a reader. But his publisher's plan to have him write a companion book to Gilbert White's *Selborne* turned him into a wonderful winter naturalist. He dropped all the season's conventional attributes and replaced them with a unique observation of plants and creatures:

Bottengoms in winter,
Charles Hall

Wednesday 2 March 1825

Found a Mavis thrushes nest with 3 eggs. These birds always build early. They make a nest like a black birds but instinct has taught them a lesson against the cold which the other has no occasion for and that is they never line their nests without wool which keeps the nests warm this early season. They always begin to sing as soon as the male blossoms of the hazel (or Trails) make their appearance and build their nests when female flowers put forth their little crimson threads at the end of the buds to receive the impregnating dust of the male dangling trails.

And in *February – a Thaw*, a long poem celebrating winter's let-up, he gives us the very essence of relief from cold. However, it is a brief happiness and all too soon the 'shepherds bend along/ Crouching to the whizzing storms'. The vivid accuracy of this always brings back to me our stumbling across ploughed fields to our grandmother's house on a February afternoon when the snowflakes were blindingly black against our small faces and our feet met with rock-hard soil. Clare's winter walkers, usually boys made to do tasks while their elders hugged the hearth, 'hirple' (limp) over the sullen fields. Should they grow up and become ploughmen, they will still have an uneven gait as one foot will be in the rut and the other above it. They will walk like land sailors. Big snows can obliterate the most familiar landscape, as they have frequently done around my farmhouse, making it difficult to know where to set foot. Clare wakes up to a snow Sahara, a featureless white into which he can only sink. His winter landscape is one of brimming fen dykes and aching trees, of water-birds and cutting winds, but above it a lark sings, as the poet does, rising beyond the seasonal limits. For me, John Clare is the peerless reminder of what we have all forgotten, or believe we have replaced for the better – ordinary winter weather. He lived through one of those 'little ice ages' – Charles Dickens being its cheerful historian – as did Samuel Pepys, years which took the true measure of winter, and against which our brief freeze-ups amid many spring-like weeks cause us to feel cheated. 'Nineteen forty-seven', 'nineteen sixty-three' we mutter: those were the days! But I think of Clare in the vast lunatic asylum with its stingy fires interminably describing snowy Helpston and its blood-warming activity, its hares, its bells, its unseasonable flowers, its 'croodling' (contracting their bodies from the cold) boys and warm girls.

Scripture gave our ancestors short shrift, seasons-wise. They do not mention spring or autumn as such, but call them seedtime and harvest. Summer is blissfully acknowledged by the poet of 'The Song of Solomon' and I had his verse from it carved on John Nash's tombstone: 'For, lo, the winter is past, the rain is over and gone, the flowers appear on the earth, the time of the singing of birds is come, and the voice of the turtle is heard in the land.' Not often is it obliterated by his beloved snow, more by lichen as it eats into the letters. Old Testament kings retire to their winter-houses and crouch over braziers. It was winter when Christ entered the Temple and was ordered to identify himself. On another occasion he spoke of the end of the world, considerately adding, 'If you try to flee from God's wrath, do not do it in the winter.' And it was the approach of winter which made St Paul ask Timothy to fetch his cloak from Troas – 'And the books, especially the parchments.' And I imagine the young man plunging through the first snows of Asia Minor.

It was the thrilling, faintly worrying smell of coming snow which disturbed us country children. There was a distinctive darkening of both sky and field, and a slight lessening of the bitter cold, and then – the fall. Let it settle! Waking to a great snowfall and to an immaculate universe printed only by birds' feet – this was the only winter we recognised.

*   *   *

One hears people say that, due to some mildness in the weather or some determined busyness on their part, they 'hardly noticed the winter'. That it was here and gone without a blast, and that, could one believe it, their garden carried through from a very late summer to an extraordinarily early spring without so much as a hint of desolation. Which I have always thought a pity. No gardener should try to dodge winter, or watch its harsh tactics with dismay. For the garden it is rest time and for the gardener it is reading time, though not for those 'what has to be done in January' kind of books. Ignore these. I read old seed catalogues, some immensely ancient like those sent from Clarence Elliott's Six Hills Nursery in 1926 to the friend who left them to me, along with other treasures, such as a run of *Gardening Illustrated* for 1932. I read Dean Hole, of course, and Margery Fish, William Robinson, E. A. Bunyard, and last winter for the first time, Elizabeth von Arnim.

The latter amazed me by her finding the scent of hyacinths 'wanting in chastity', whereas coming down to a wintry old room in which bowls of hyacinth have been confined all night is for me among the purest enchantments of the season. For Elizabeth they are a 'smell' which is a winter make-do because 'in December one cannot afford to be fastidious.' All the same, no one better relished and understood the purposes of a garden in winter. These were the days when the cold of indoors made the cold of outdoors simply a variation of chilliness and when one dressed for the entrance hall. So at Nassenheide, her Pomeranian castle, both garden and house were, for Elizabeth, united in wintriness. As they were so for three months of every year, she had to be positive about it. She planned beds and got carried away when it came to ordering things, such as marrow-seed and primrose-roots from England, these according to her being unknown in 1898 Prussia. What with her frozen soil and what with some of her remarks, one certainly feels the ice of Nassenheide in winter.

Each of us possesses a garden situation which invites a repeated question. Mine is, 'Do you ever get snowed-in?' Of course, I say. It is obvious, really. I live in a hollow and snow naturally fills it up, though not often. But it happens, and although taken aback by the immensity and beauty of it, I set the 'drifts' routine in motion. This primarily involves checking that I can get to the road by way of the high field instead of the

SIX HILLS SEEDS

Six Hills Seeds are so Pushing!

CLARENCE ELLIOTT, LTD.
SIX HILLS NURSERY
STEVENAGE - HERTS

John Nash illustration
for the 1929 catalogue

always blocked lane, marvelling that the various power lines, now swollen into thick white ropes, and hanging low in great loops, do not snap, rescuing here and there a shrub from its intolerable burden of snow platters and trying to convince the cat that, as the prophet said, all this, like everything else, is only for a time. So brace up. It was while lunching in the garden last summer – that epic summer! – that the American friend asked me, rather casually, as people do when they are certain of the excellence of something which they are about to recommend, had I read Whittier's *Snowbound*? No. It is about a New England farming family being snowed-in and then thawed-out during the winter of 1866, and I doubt if any other writer has described the curtailment which winter brings to plants, folk, animals and work so movingly.

But epic winters are thin on the ground these days and the garden only disappears in blizzards once or twice a decade. For the most part it retains, January after January, a stark visibility, becoming open and spacious, like familiar old rooms when the clutter is removed and the simple lineaments of their basic furnishings are revealed. I look through beds and hedges, instead of into them, and am in a world of sticks. Here and there a daisy persists in the sodden grass. Premature digging will occasionally disturb a bulb and I am momentarily taken aback by the white and green growth. Winter is dissolution on the surface and astounding vitality under it. I may loaf but the garden doesn't. The east coast wind tears across it, and the cold is dreadful. Unbelievably, since one prides oneself on getting out in any weather, there are days when one cannot. Through the window I can see hellebores looking quite comfortable and my neighbour's field, taken out of corn for 'set aside', gleaming with the grass which was sown last September, and looking far tidier than my lawn. Keeping off the grass when it is frozen takes me on unusual garden walks. Frost creates its own inimitable stillness and the bare lilacs, hazels, oaks and particularly the ash trees, during late winter, are immersed in their annual process of not stirring, not giving so much as a tremor to show their strong inner greening. Not so the *Garrya elliptica* (named after young Michael Garry of the Hudson's Bay Company), whose cascade of budding catkins and dense crisp leaves form such an elegant accompaniment to snow.

It would be wrong to say that the dark short days and the mud, and at times the piercing East Anglian cold, do not occasionally override my philosophical tolerance, and even love, of winter. There is a bleakness which is about the seasonal world at rock bottom so far as human nature is concerned, yet something which I wouldn't miss. How the old northern European settlers here dreaded such winter days! For a terrible moment they doubted the return of the spring and it made them black with pessimism. It would have been February, when they had eaten everything preservable. Hunger makes one feel very low. Rough clues to their existence turn up in the icy fields around the garden and cling to place-names, saying 'I was here'. The villagers used to say that they saw them (or some ancient presence or other) in the dag, the misty dews, shimmering and soaking. 'Shut the door', they used to shout when one called on them, and it wasn't only to keep out the cold.

Good gardeners prepare themselves for bad winters – or any winter. They are not easy times for body or spirit, nor can they be escaped. Their pleasures, as Vita Sackville-West found, have to be taken along with their pain.

> Still may you with your frozen fingers cut
> Treasures of Winter, if you planted well;
> The Winter-sweet against a sheltering wall,
> Waxen, Chinese and drooping bell;
> Strange in its colour, almond in its smell;
> And the Witch-hazel, *Hamamelis mollis*,
> That comes before its leaf on naked bough,
> Torn ribbons frayed, of yellow and maroon,
> And sharp of scent in frosty English air . . .
> Gardener, if you listen, listen well:
> Plant for your winter pleasure, when the months
> Dishearten; plant to find a fragile note
> Touched from the brittle violin of frost.

The Garden, 1946